More Praise

"*Coming Alive* is one of the most significant books of meditations I have ever read, and I've read many. Harper's reflections on biblical texts are both simple and profound, and his one-sentence prayers at the end of each day are memorable for their wisdom, insight, and brevity. There is a freshness of perspective and a willingness to be vulnerable in these words. They are expansive and universal, reminding us that Jesus is for all with no exceptions. Harper invites us to come alive and experience new freedom in Christ in place of being chained to a rigid religiosity that drains the life out of us."

—Darrell Whiteman, founder of Global Development, Seattle, WA; retired professor of cultural anthropology, Asbury Theological Seminary, Wilmore, KY

"This is a devotional gem. The entries are short and meaty enough to focus readers on what matters most. The life that oozes from each entry points to the Life we all need day by day!"

—Thomas Jay Oord, theologian; author of *Open and Relational Theology*

"*Coming Alive* is an excellent and timely book! Dr. Harper makes scripture relatable and offers remarkable reflections based on his pastoral work, academic trajectory, as well as personal experiences. I cannot think of any devotional book that provides such a holistic approach. May God lead us from devotion to action, as Dr. Harper suggests, as we read these pages."

—Hugo Magallanes, Associate Dean for Academic Affairs, associate professor of Christianity and cultures, SMU Perkins School of Theology, Dallas, TX

"With simplicity, brevity, and clarity, this is a beautiful daily guide to prayer."

—Elaine A. Heath, theologian, consultant, and author of *The Healing Practice of Celebration, Five Means of Grace: Experience God's Love the Wesleyan Way*, and others from Abingdon Press

"Sometimes, at a particular moment, a devotional book intersects your life, and you learn its arrival was not a coincidence. The words of Steve Harper's *Coming Alive* leaped off the page and headed straight for my soul! Thus is a devotional already marked up and awaiting its second reading."

—Harold Ivan Smith, scholar, author, and expert on death and grief

"For decades many of us have known that we can trust Steve Harper to guide us. Theologian, theological educator, pastor, and church leader, Steve has a gift for expressing the deepest truths of the faith in ways that lead us to better understanding and more vibrant witness. Here's a book for everyday Christians that equips them for daily Christian life, an enlivening exploration of the way of Christ that is sure to make you more fully alive to Christ."

—Will Willimon, professor of the practice of Christian ministry, Duke Divinity School; retired United Methodist bishop; and author of *Preachers Dare: Hearing God in the Sermon* from Abingdon Press

"The constant compulsion to seek cultural relevance has resulted in a fast-food theology that does not satisfy the hunger for lasting spiritual nourishment, felt especially by younger generations of Christians. That is why *Coming Alive* is such a timely and needed book. It provides informative and inspiring answers to the deadening effects of spiritual undernourishment. Contrary to 'pop spirituality,' it offers a treasure trove of gospel truth, packaged in small, accessible bites that enable us to taste and savor the wisdom of the Lord, not once but time and again. I feel sure that readers of every age will befriend this book and reap its benefits."

—Susan Muto, Dean, Epiphany Academy of Formative Spirituality, Pittsburgh, PA

"Like Steve Harper himself, this book is a treasure trove. Each day brings a gem of insight into the scripture reading that is memorable, portable, and applicable. Along the way, he offers a deep dive into some of the Bible's most famous passages, eliciting new insights that reorient our thinking and behavior. This is a book worth owning, recommending, gifting, and revisiting, year after year."

—Magrey R. deVega, senior pastor, Hyde Park United Methodist Church, Tampa, FL; author of *The Bible Year: A Journey through Scripture in 365 Days* from Abingdon Press

"Use these daily meditations to allow God to speak God's life into your life. And expect a year of spiritual transformation. When Steve Harper speaks, I listen, expecting to hear a message through him, from God."

—Daryl L. Smith, 5Q coach and equipping crafter; cell group creator and leader coach

"Consider this an invitation to gather with Steve for a metamorphic conversation five days of every week about truly coming alive."

—Michael Beck, pastor, Wildwood United Methodist Church, Wildwood, FL

STEVE HARPER

Foreword by Brian McLaren

Coming Alive

Daily Meditations
for Spiritual Renewal

Nashville

COMING ALIVE:
DAILY MEDITATIONS FOR SPIRITUAL RENEWAL

Copyright © 2022 by Abingdon Press

Library of Congress Control Number: 2022945356

ISBN: 978-1-7910-2786-5

MANUFACTURED IN THE UNITED STATES OF AMERICA

Contents

Foreword

Through much of my life, I have benefited from books of daily meditations. Whether with breakfast, at midday, or before bed, they have helped me center myself and give me something to ponder, celebrate, or savor. My favorite daily meditations have had four characteristics.

First, they have a connection to Scripture—evoking a story or short quotation or even a single word. Second, they offer a reflection on that Scripture, something for me to return to throughout the day as a source of inspiration, encouragement, or challenge. Third, they offer a short prompt to prayer, inviting me to "center down" (as Howard Thurman used to say) and enjoy "conscious contact with God" (as The Twelve Steps say). And fourth, they have been short enough to leave me wanting more and substantial enough to give me something to keep thinking about.

I'm so glad Steve Harper's new book *Coming Alive* is now available. It beautifully fulfills all four of these characteristics. Not only that, but it also focuses in on the real core of the spiritual life: not dogma, not rules and regulations, not duties or guilt, not pressure or obligation—but life, life to the full, what I like to call *aliveness*. Here's how I described it in my book *We Make the Road by Walking*:

What we all want is pretty simple, really. We want to be alive. To feel alive. Not just to exist but to thrive, to live out loud, walk tall, breathe free. We want to be less lonely, less exhausted, less conflicted or afraid . . . more awake, more grateful, more energized and purposeful. We capture this kind of mindful, overbrimming life in terms like well-being, shalom, blessedness, wholeness, harmony, life to the full, and aliveness. . . . The quest for aliveness is the best thing about religion, I think. It's what we're hoping for when we pray. It's why we gather, celebrate, eat, abstain, attend, practice, sing, and contemplate. When people say "I'm spiritual," what they mean, I think, is simple: "I'm seeking aliveness."[1]

Here's what I recommend. Keep this book somewhere you'll encounter it every day—on your bedside table, on your kitchen table, in the front seat of your car, in your briefcase or backpack. Keep a pencil or pen nearby so that you can jot down the date after you read. You may want to underline something or write a short note to yourself too. Keep it simple. Your notes and underlinings will be there to remind you later what struck you on your first reading.

This simple practice can be like a simple rendezvous each day—with God, with your own soul—to help you live your life to the full, day by day by day.

Enjoy!

Brian D. McLaren

Preface

Every particle of our being desires to live and ever-increasingly to come alive in new ways. From the moment of conception, the life-urge is paramount. The God of Life creates everyone and everything to live.

The Bible confirms this. If I had to summarize the biblical message in one word, I would say *life*. I would go to John 10:10. After that, I would point to our universal desire to live well, and the many ways we seek to thrive, not just survive. I have written about this previously in a book titled *Life in Christ*.[1]

In this book, I continue the theme of life, but I write about it in a different way—as a series of meditations intended to be used over the course of a year. People have occasionally asked me, "Have you written a book of daily meditations?" They mean something like Oswald Chambers's *My Utmost for His Highest*, L. B. Cowman's *Streams in the Desert*, or another such book that provides a year's worth of readings. Up to now, my answer has been no.

But obviously, this book turns my response into a yes. I hope it is a divine yes. I have written it from my sense that abundant living unfolds little by little. Considering it in day-sized portions aids our experiencing of it. Most of my insights have come in small amounts. This book captures some of them, and I offer them to you in the hope that you will find them to be life-giving.

For sixty years I have begun most days reading and reflecting on the Bible and other inspirational writing. This practice has been key to my spiritual formation. The "quiet time" has been, as E. Stanley Jones described it, a listening post from which I receive my marching orders for the day—directives that move me into abundant living. I hope that as you read these meditations, they will fan the flame of love in your heart that causes you to come alive in new ways.

Steve Harper

Introduction

I understand this book in keeping with Thomas Merton's understanding of his written meditations. I want you to read my book the way he hoped people would read his:

> The purpose of a book of meditations is to teach you how to think and not to do your thinking for you. Consequently, if you pick up a book and simply read it through, you are wasting your time. As soon as any thought stimulates your mind or heart, you can put the book down because your meditation has begun. To think that you are somehow obliged to follow the author of the book to his [or her, or their] own particular conclusion would be a great mistake. It may happen that his [her, their] conclusion does not apply to you. God may want you to end up somewhere else. [God] may have planned to give you quite a different grace from the one the author suggests you need.[1]

I hope you will read this book that way. I hope you will spend more time with your thoughts than mine. You may want to keep a companion notebook and write your own meditations in relation to these. Let the written words "come alive" in you . . . and be enacted through you.

Using This Book

I have designed the format to encourage your own reflection. In the end, what you experience is more important than what I have written. So, each day's meditation is short.

I encourage you to keep a journal as you read, capturing the insights and inspirations you receive.

I have written five meditations per week. This gives you some flexibility, which is important as you set out on this yearlong journey. I want you to be able to miss a day or two if need be. I like Joyce Rupp's idea that we should "walk in a relaxed manner" in the spiritual life. Giving you leeway each week will help you do that.

You may want to use this book in a small group setting. At the end of the book I have a suggested guide for group meetings.

In Week Fifty-Two I "pass the baton" to Brian McLaren's book *We Make the Road by Walking*, and invite you to make it the next leg of your journey. Also, at the end of this book I suggest other resources.

I hope these features will help foster your receptivity, appreciation, enrichment, and enactment of what you find in this book.

Daily Meditations

Week One, Day 1

Read John 10:10

If we were to ask Jesus why he came, he would repeat what he said in the verse for today. If he came to give us life, then letting him do that is the most important thing we can do. We are made for abundant life.

The Greeks had two words for life: *bios* and *zoé*. *Bios* is our physical life and everything we associate with it. *Zoé* is another quality of life, what Jesus called "abundant life." Both forms of life are sacred, and the spiritual life is an honoring of both. But abundant living—*zoé* life—is living in sync with God's will. *Zoé* life is called "eternal life" to distinguish it from earthly (*bios*) life. But it is not life deferred until eternity; it can begin now (Romans 6:4). We sometimes refer to it as "life in Christ" (see 2 Corinthians 5:17) or "[being] guided by the Spirit" (Galatians 5:16-25).

The point is this: there is a difference between existing (*bios*) and living (*zoé*). God's invitation is an invitation to Life. God offers us *zoé* life.

Prayer: God, I want to live, not simply exist. I believe you can help me to do this. Amen.

Week One, Day 2

Read Psalm 37:25

When I go to the grocery store, I check the expiration date on certain items. I want to be sure the food I purchase will stay fresh until it's eaten. God's grace and love is not like that. It has no expiration date. *Zoé* life is fresh in every season of life. David writes about this.

We have different seasons of life: spring, summer, fall, and winter.[1] But no season is devoid of life. Life simply takes a different form in each season. Abundant life is present from start to finish. *Zoé* life is present and active in every part of life.

As John Wesley was dying, among his final words were these, "The best of all is, God is with us." He was eighty-nine years old. He had lived the reality of today's psalm. We can too.

Prayer: God, awaken me to the reality that you are with me always. Help me to live abundantly in every stage of my life. Amen.

Week One, Day 3

Read 2 Corinthians 6:2

We have a sense of past, present, and future. But in reality, we only live in the present moment. We must learn to live here and now, not there and later.

Henri Nouwen wrote about this, observing that we cannot live in the past; it is gone. When we attempt to do so, we fall prey to "oughts." Nor can we live in the future; it is not here yet. When we try to do so, we are controlled by "ifs." Neither of these options is life-giving because we only live today, in the "is" of reality.[2]

When Moses asked to know God's name, the only name God gave him was I Am (Exodus 3:14). Here is the ultimate sign that we live abundantly in the present Nouwen moment. It's the only place where we can.

Prayer: God, tune my heart to see you, hear you, and respond to you here and now. Help me experience the reality and joy of living in the present moment. Amen.

Week One, Day 4

Read Matthew 12:1-23

Jesus ignored laws that ignored needs. Jesus broke laws that broke people. And he got in trouble for it. Legalists are predisposed to push back because "obeying the law" is their highest virtue. But for Jesus, "doing good" was the ultimate value (Acts 10:38).

When laws reflect goodness, we obey them. When they do not, we resist them. When we resist unjust laws, we do so not because we disrespect law and order, but because we recognize that the law in question violates God's law (which is love) and order (which is righteousness).

Obedience gives life because it expresses Life. Obedience to not-Life rules and regulations is not true obedience. It is selling our souls to "the kingdoms of this world" rather than devoting them to the kingdom of God.

Prayer: God, today I want to be truly obedient, giving you my utmost for your highest. Amen.

Week One, Day 5

Read Matthew 25:31-46

Reflect: Jesus never defined life by our affirmations, but by our actions. Lofty declarations do not prove our genuineness; concrete behaviors do. Moreover, it is in the presence or absence of compassion that we see Jesus or fail to do so.

Love is proven by loving care. Righteousness is demonstrated in relationships. Character is conveyed through conduct. We must be doers of the word, not just hearers of it (James 1:22). The fruit of the Spirit (Galatians 5:22-23) is a seamless tapestry of inward qualities and outward manifestations.

We turn love into loving when we recognize that the incarnation is not an isolated story about Jesus; it is a universal pattern for us. God intends that the Word becomes flesh in everyone, everywhere, and in every age. We will never become gods or rival Jesus as the incarnation of the Son of God, but we will become human and reflect Christlikeness.

Prayer: God, convert my declarations into deeds. Amen.

⚓⚓

Week Two, Day 1

Read Matthew 20:27-28

The higher we ascend into pride, the farther we move away from Jesus. He redefined greatness, calling it servanthood and modeling it in the upper room on the night of his betrayal (see John 13:2-17). The way of descent is the way into greatness.

Almost everything in the world tempts us into superiority. The working definition of greatness is supremacy: better than, stronger than, richer than, smarter than, larger than, more than . . . the "others." Jesus eliminated comparative, binary judgmentalism and leveled the playing field by showing compassion to everyone and caring for anyone in need.

The way of life is the way of renunciation, not ruling. It is the way of humility, not hubris. It is the way of befriending, not belittling. It is the way of noticing, not ignoring. It is the way of identification, not separation. Greatness is low-decibel love, not high-volume egotism.

Prayer: God, lead me downward, into your greatness—the greatness that gives light and life to all. Amen.

Week Two, Day 2

Read Psalm 146:5-10

God is the maker of heaven and earth, and as our Creator, God has a clear vision for life. It is God's intention that justice (fairness, equity, and inclusion) is given to all. The oppressed, the starving, prisoners, blind people, and those bent low (put down, neglected, abused), immigrants, widows and orphans (the marginalized and needy) are particular recipients of God's faithful love.

They are also the ones to whom we look in order to see if we are living in keeping with God's plan. That is, do we show compassion for and give specific care to the ones described here? Fallen-world leaders and the governments they create neglect these people, enriching the rich at the expense of the poor, and enhancing the few to the detriment of the many.

We are called to live differently, exposing imperialism and expressing righteousness in our words and deeds. As St. Francis put it, we are instruments of God's peace.

Prayer: God, give me a heart of love for "the least of these." Amen.

Week Two, Day 3

Read Matthew 3:1-2

Who is your John the Baptist? That is, the one who prepared the way of the Lord for you? I have asked this question many times over the years, and people always have those they can name. I do too. Looking back, we can identify folks who influenced us prior to our becoming followers of Jesus.

Most of these people were much appreciated, but sometimes they were people who frustrated or agitated us at the time, like John the Baptist did. On a few occasions people have named their John the Baptist as someone who made them want to turn and go in another direction! But now they recognize that even those persons were preparing the way.

It is possible to have an original and isolated experience of God, but most of the time our experiences are the result of previous ones. God uses the past to "prepare the way of the Lord" for us today. And even our present experiences are doorways into new ones tomorrow.

Prayer: God, I give thanks for the people who prepared the way of the Lord for me. Use me to be a "John the Baptist" for others. Amen.

Week Two, Day 4

Read Luke 12:35-40

Readiness is not so much having everything in shape, as it is being alert. A spirituality focused on having our ducks in a row can deflect our attentiveness away from God onto ourselves. We end up cultivating scrupulosity and calling it spirituality. When we do this, we put our performance ahead of God's grace.

Jesus did not ask the servants to be perfect; he asked them to be watchful. And more, he asked them to be celebratory, not anxious. Scrupulosity can never relax. It always thinks, "I have not done enough. I should be doing more."

Spiritual attentiveness is restful because it is trustful. We wait for God with a sense of expectancy, not trepidation. We wait for God knowing that God's "arrival" will be for our good. We wait with hope.

Prayer: God, I am looking for you with anticipation, not anxiety. Amen.

Week Two, Day 5

Read Luke 5:15-16

A college friend went on to become the captain for a major airline. Once when I visited him, I remarked that flying must have become second nature to him. "Oh, no!" he replied, "We never stop following the printed protocols. We never ignore the pattern."

His words attach to today's reading. Jesus is the pattern. We must never stop paying attention to him and go it alone. Instead, we follow him every day of our lives. Jesus's pattern is clear: working and resting, engaging and withdrawing, doing and being.

Too often we ignore the pattern and lose the rhythm. We fall prey to activism, which Thomas Merton called a form of violence.[3] When we stop following Jesus's pattern, we harm ourselves (e.g., fatigue) and others (e.g., unreal expectations). But when we follow his pattern, we thrive and so do those around us.

Prayer: God, teach me to follow the pattern and never to ignore it. Amen.

❧❧

Week Three, Day 1

Read 1 John 2:27

Today's reading is challenging, but also necessary. It is challenging because, at first glance, it seems to teach a spirituality (an "anointing") that eliminates the need to have teachers. But that is not its meaning. Rather, John is talking about a maturation that creates a radical dependency on Christ. John is saying that we are to be guided by Christ; egotism not ethnocentrism.

The "anointing" is not spiritual independence, but rather reliance on Christ. We receive our marching orders from him. We do not sell our souls to anyone, any group, or anything. The "anointing" is the renunciation of ourselves to God that Jesus described in the first beatitude (Matthew 5:3) and which Paul called being a "living sacrifice" (Romans 12:1).

The risen Christ dwells in us (John 15:4). That's the "anointing." We never outgrow the need for this. What we are invited to abandon is "group think" where a community becomes a substitute for the Spirit. The "anointing" is not a superiority, it is a surrender.

Prayer: God, I belong to you alone. Amen.

Week Three, Day 2

Read Proverbs 18:13

A Buddhist monk was asked to comment on something that had happened a thousand years ago. The monk replied, "I am unable to say anything about that." When asked why, the monk replied, "Not enough time has passed for me to have a point of view about it."

The monk's comment seems odd in a world where people too often answer before they listen. It seems wrongheaded in a sound bite environment that exists on instant gratification. But his response comes from a different place; it comes from the recognition that perspective takes time, that there is a difference between giving an answer and providing wisdom.

We need people in our lives who model patience. We need to become comfortable saying, "I need time to think about that." We must learn there is a difference between a quick reply and a good answer.

Prayer: God, train me to go first to my thoughts rather than to my mouth. Amen.

Week Three, Day 3

Read 2 Peter 3:8

At first glance, this verse seems enigmatic, but when converted into contemporary language, it communicates a truth we need to see, "In the present moment we have all the time in the world." This is Peter's way of saying what we find elsewhere in scripture: the sufficiency of the present moment.

Whatever we need can happen here and now. Nothing need be deferred to "there" or "later." Nothing is lost to the past or postponed to the future. God is patiently present right now, right here, ready to do more for us than we can ask or imagine (Ephesians 3:20).

The cliché that says "Opportunity knocks only once" is not true. It knocks again and again. Jesus said that he stands at our door knocking, and if we open the door of our lives to him, he will have fellowship with us (Revelation 3:20). The present moment is pregnant with possibility.

Prayer: God, I look neither backward nor forward to find life. I look right here, right now—where you are. Amen.

Week Three, Day 4

Read Luke 12:49

When I was a child, I enjoyed playing with a magnifying glass. On sunshiny day I would gather dry grass and leaves, and set them on fire by using the magnifying glass to concentrate light into a beam. Concentrated light ignites a fire.

God is light (1 John 1:5). That light was concentrated in the incarnation. The Word became flesh (John 1:14). Jesus was the light of the world (John 8:12). The concentrated light of God in Jesus ignites a fire in us—often called a "fire of love."

Blaise Pascal experienced this fire and wrote, "The year of grace 1654. Monday, 23 November, feast of Saint Clement, Pope and Martyr, and of others in the Martyrology. Eve of Saint Chrysogonus, Martyr and others. From about half past ten in the evening until half past midnight, Fire!" He went on to say it was a transforming experience of joy and peace. It is the experience Christ, God's magnifying glass, continues to give, his concentrated light that shines on us.

Prayer: God, I submit the "grass and leaves" of my life to you—fire! Amen.

Week Three, Day 5

Read Acts 14:17

When a gentle rain falls, the earth seems to calm down. All is quiet except for the sound the rain makes as it strikes leaves and runs down roofs. And for a little while we experience the blessing of God through rainfall.

Nature has been called the first Bible. Before we had scripture, we had creation. Our ancestors were more in tune with it, more in awe of it, and more caring toward it than we are today. But on days when the rain falls and "all nature sings," we recover our primal oneness with all things. We are connected with the cosmic cycle of life, from which we derive our being.

A rainy day is a good day to be like the earth, receiving the grace of God just as the soil welcomes water. The blessing of rain is the reminder that we are alive with God's life.

Prayer; God, make my soul the soil into which the rain of your love soaks. Amen.

❦

Week Four, Day 1

Read Mark 1:17

We know we are called to be disciples, and we can study the meaning of the word (e.g., follower, learner) to gain insight into what it means. But how to do it is another question. It is one Jesus answered in the phrase "fish for people." He was talking to fishermen. Fishermen know how to fish. Jesus was saying that discipleship is doing what you already know how to do, and doing it for him.

What do you already know how to do? What are you already doing? Make that the instrument of your discipleship. Your function is your format. Your place of livelihood is your location. Your routine is your role. Fishermen fish. We do what we are, and we do it for Jesus.

We all can gain further information about being a disciple. But we do not have to guess what the instrument is, or wonder when it will come along. The instrument of our discipleship is our life as we live it every day. Fishermen fish. What do you do? Do it for Jesus.

Prayer: God, I am a _____. I will do it for you! Amen.

Week Four, Day 2

Read Psalm 126:6

When we are in the midst of grief, it seems it will never end. Interestingly, the Bible doesn't teach that grief can be ended. It teaches that it can be transformed. The psalmist spoke of the transformation as "going out." Grief is transformed when we turn outward.

This is not the same as "time heals all things." Time doesn't heal anything, but how we use time makes a difference. The psalmist describes our use of time as "carrying seed." If in our grief we go out of ourselves (and the tendency to "go in," which grief compels) and invest in others, we can return with joy and a bountiful harvest.

It may be the harvest of letting others care for us. It may be the harvest of walking in a park and breathing fresh air. It may be the harvest of small talk with a friend over coffee. Or it may be serving someone who needs help. We sow, we harvest. We go out with tears, we return with joy. Our grief is not over, but it is no longer overwhelming.

Prayer: God, when grief comes, I will not turn inward to it, I will turn outward to life. Amen.

Week Four, Day 3

Read Joshua 1:3

How many steps do we take in a year? If we use the 10,000-steps-a-day cardio formula, it would be 3,650,000. But even if we are not in the pep-step crowd, the number is still in the neighborhood of a million.

Laid alongside today's verse, we are given an amazing promise: every step we take will be in the presence of God. God's word to Joshua was a precursor to the idea of Emmanuel, "God with us," no matter where we go.

Some of our steps are routine and predictable. Others take us off our beaten path into unexplored territory. Some steps are on smooth, level ground. But other steps are a rocky, uphill climb. Some steps are a stroll, others are a sprint, and still others are a struggle. Some journeys refresh us, others wear us out. But no matter how easy or difficult our steps may be, we never walk alone.

Prayer: God, I do not have to shout for you to hear me, for you are by my side each step of the way. Thank you. Amen.

Week Four, Day 4

Read Matthew 7:14

We read the words *narrow way* and we think "narrowness"— a moral statement equivalent to telling someone, "Watch your business. Stay on the straight and narrow. God is not pleased when you deviate from the right path." But that is not what Jesus meant.

As a Wisdom teacher, he was referring to what Buddhism, Taoism, Native American religions, and (later) Anglicanism call the Middle Way. It is the way that avoids extremes and excess (the "broad way"), and walks in moderation. It shuns the edges, where differences are emphasized, and travels down the center where commonalities are recognized. Jesus said that few find this way, because we are too easily and often given over to divisions and judgments.

He essentially defined the narrow way in verse 13—the one we call the Golden Rule. We walk the narrow/Middle Way when we treat others the way we want to be treated by them. This way of life sums up the Law and the Prophets.

Prayer: God, guide me to walk on the middle way, your way. Amen.

Week Four, Day 5

Read Psalm 8:1

Recall the most spectacular sunrise or sunset you've ever seen. Remember as many of the thoughts and feelings you had in that moment as you can. Even then, David wrote that God's glory exceeds it. It's higher than (above and beyond) the heavens, more spectacular than anything we can imagine.

Nature has been called "the first Bible" by many Christians. That's because nature revealed God billions of years before scripture was ever written. From time immemorial, people have been drawn into the divine through their experiences in nature. Nature is a wonderful window through which to look in order to see God.

But it is only a window. The glory (reality and magnificence) of God is more than a moment that takes our breath away, it is the sense that every moment is a God moment—that all creation is aglow with God's light. That includes you! It includes everyone!

Prayer: God, give me a sense of yourself that's so large I cannot take it, so encompassing that I cannot imagine myself or anyone else outside of it. Amen.

Week Five, Day 1

Read Philippians 1:9-10

Discernment is living with insight. It is a mark of wisdom. It does not come quickly and easily, but neither is it confusing and complicated. Paul connects it with love and knowledge. Discernment is putting what we know in the service of love. Two things emerge from this.

First, we recognize that discernment is a way of fulfilling the two great commandments. It is asking, "How can I love God and others in this moment?" Discernment is insight applied to life. The second thing is that we do not have to wait until some future time when we "know more" or "see things better." We can use the knowledge we have for the glory of God and the good of others. In fact, it is in using what we have that we grow in love and knowledge (Matthew 13:12).

Brother Lawrence wrote the items compiled in *The Practice of the Presence of God* in the seventeenth century, and it remains a devotional classic. In it he said, "We can do little things for God." This is what we do when we turn love and knowledge into action in the present moment.

Prayer: God, I put what I know at your service. Amen.

Week Five, Day 2

Read Genesis 1:27-28

Once in a while someone tries to defend something they have said or done by saying, "Don't blame me, I'm only human." At first glance, the words sound reasonable. After all, everyone makes mistakes. Nobody's perfect.

But taking a closer look, the words are simply not true. In our moments of weakness and failure, the problem is not that we're human. The problem is that we were not human enough. Careless and harmful words are subhuman.

To be human is to be made in the image of God. In our humanity we are like God in many respects. Our sins and faults are not due to our humanity, but rather are expressions of our inhumanity. Our first call in scripture is to be human. Our failure to be human is the problem. Humanity is God's highest idea, just a little lower than the angels (Psalm 8:5). When we speak and act inappropriately, humanity is not something to blame as a justification; it is something to claim as a liberation.

Prayer: God, I will not blame my humanity for my dilemma, I will claim it for my deliverance. Amen.

Week Five, Day 3

Read Acts 17:6

As Christianity spread beyond Jerusalem, the disciples were accused of turning the world upside down. And that is surely how it must have felt among those for whom the status quo had become a sacred cow. It is a charge the early Christians did not deny, and for doing so they suffered intensely (see Hebrews 11).

But the fact is, these witnesses and martyrs were not turning the world upside down; they were turning it right side up. The fall in Genesis 3 turned the world upside down. So, when Jesus and his followers overturned things, they were returning them to their proper position.

Restoration is always a threat to those for whom "the system is the solution." Fallen-world leaders have it like they want it, and they never take kindly to resistance. But the actions of the first disciples are needed today. God continues to call us to turn things right side up.

Prayer: God, give me wisdom to know what I can help to overturn and the courage to do so. Amen.

Week Five, Day 4

Read Psalm 37:7-8

Getting upset may seem like a sign that we are concerned about something, but it is more nearly an indication that something had taken hold of us. The Hebrew word pictures us being on fire, and not in a good way. When we are upset, something is consuming us, rather than us conquering it.

It is easy to become upset when so many things are happening that are wrong. That's why we must understand that anger and rage weaken us, at the very time when we need to be strong. Fretting and fighting are two ways of expending our energy. Fretting turns it on ourselves in a destructive way. Fighting turns it on the object in a transforming way.

Those we name who gave/give themselves to nonviolent resistance were/are fighters not fretters. Rather than getting upset, they get up. Rather than being overcome by evil, they overcome evil with good (Romans 12:21). In doing so, they use the energy of concern in constructive ways. This is our call too.

Prayer: God, I will not get upset, I will get up. I choose to be a fighter, not a fretter. Amen.

Week Five, Day 5

Read John 5:30

Jesus engaged in many works, but he only had one work. Like us, he had a lot of things to do, but he did them all in relation to one purpose—to do God's will. He spoke of this numerous times in John's Gospel, indicating that he was nourished through the doing of God's will.[4]

When our desire is singular, every activity becomes a means of fulfilling it. Every qualifier falls by the wayside: for example, large/small, public/private, and so on. When we have one mission, every moment is an opportunity to carry it out.

Singularity begets comprehensiveness because we no longer have to size up the situation before deciding whether or not to live our faith. Spirituality is natural, not contrived. Every moment is a God-moment.

Prayer: God, I want to do your will . . . here and now. Amen.

Week Six, Day 1

Read Romans 8:26-27 and Hebrews 7:25

What is Christ doing right now? Twice we are told that he is praying for us. Of course, what this means exactly is a mystery, but what a beautiful and powerful idea it is!

When the risen Christ ascended into heaven, he did not cease to know about us, love us, or care for us. He became our intercessor. He is praying for us this very moment. Every second of our lives is saturated with prayer, from the Holy Trinity itself!

Sometimes when we are facing a challenge or going through a hard time, we will say to a friend, "Pray for me." And that's something friends are always ready and willing to do. Christ's ongoing intercession is evidence that when we sing "What a friend we have in Jesus," it's true!

Prayer: God, today I will not say, "Pray for me." Today I say, "Thanks for praying for me." Amen.

Week Six, Day 2

Read Acts 9:2

Before they were called Christians, Jesus's disciples were described as belonging to the Way.[5] This is likely due to Jesus's declaration, "I am the way" (John 14:6). His identity became the initial identity of his disciples.

Very likely it was an indication that Jesus was in the larger flow of religious history, with the most obvious rootage being the Tao, which means "way." Far from watering down the faith, calling disciples followers of the Way meant they were Big Story people living expansively. Following the universal Christ, they lived deep and wide.

In the same way today, our witness is strengthened when we show we belong to the Way. We live from abundance, not scarcity; from spaciousness, not sectarianism. We manifest addition, not subtraction; enrichment, not diminishment. We are alive with Life.

Prayer: God, I claim my faith at its highest peak. I follow the one who is the Way. Amen.

Week Six, Day 3

Read Galatians 2:20

When we live in Christ, we no longer live egotistically. Writing of his own experience, Paul described it this way, "I no longer live, but Christ lives in me." Life in Christ delivers us from self-centeredness.

Thomas Merton wrote extensively about Christ's freeing us from the false self.[6] The false self is not all bad. The problem is that it fosters self-gratification rather than God-glorification. We live with the question, "What's in it for me?" as our guiding principle.

Life in Christ puts God at the center. Our self is not eliminated, it is relocated. The self is not canceled out, it is consecrated (Romans 12:1). We desire to do God's will more than anything else.

Prayer: God, I want every part of my life to be a hallelujah. Amen.

Week Six, Day 4

Read Psalm 34:19

Our faith and spirituality do not exempt us from having problems of all kinds. The book of Job, perhaps the oldest book in the Bible, teaches this. David wrote of it again in today's reading. Jesus suffered, and so did many of the first Christians.

The witness of Christians across the ages is not that they have no difficulties, but that they are not defeated by them. Sometimes our sufferings are intense (e.g., Paul's testimony in 2 Corinthians 4:8-9), but we never experience any hardship outside the reach of God's grace.

Faith does not prevent problems; it provides strength to face them. The strength is the presence of God, who is with us no matter how dark things become (Psalm 23:4). Jesus's final promise was, "I myself will be with you every day (Matthew 28:20).

Prayer: God, I will not deny my pain when I am hurting, but neither will I discount your presence to help me get through it. Amen.

Week Six, Day 5

Read 1 Corinthians 15:14

These words from Paul reveal that he did not see Jesus's resurrection as a one-time event; he recognized it as a universal pattern. It is a pattern we see in the cosmos, one we participate in as human beings in the creation.

I am the oldest member of my immediate family. My great-grandmother on my father's side was still alive when I was born, and I have childhood memories of visits with her. But one by one, my forebears died. On that limb of our family tree, I am next in line to go!

But are they "dead and gone"? And is that the summary phrase of my life, or yours? Paul says no. The picture of Christ's resurrection is a portrait of ours as well. We are heading for "the mystery we call heaven."[7] Our faith is not in vain.

Prayer: God, I follow Christ's lead—into eternity. Amen.

Week Seven, Day 1

Read John 15:1-8

How close can we get to God? People answer the question in different ways. Jesus answered it this way: we can get as close to God as a branch gets to a vine.

Made in the image of God (Genesis 1:26-27), we are connected to God in a way that preserves the necessary God-human distinction, while proclaiming an intimate union. In the reading Jesus says the connection is life-giving, continuous, and fruitful. A bit further, he added that it is joyous (15:11), and earlier he called it abundant life (John 10:10).

In short, it is the kind of life for which we are made. We are never more alive than when we are alive in Christ.

Prayer: God, I am close to you because I am in Christ. I am where you want me, and where I want to be. Amen.

Week Seven, Day 2

Read 2 Corinthians 5:17-19

When I became a Christian, I became part of a group that had "life verses" taken from scripture. I was encouraged to find one for myself. Early on, I found the three verses in today's reading. I have continued to call them my "life verses" for nearly sixty years. Today begins a series of meditations in which I want to bear witness to their influence upon my life.

The first note is that of universal invitation. It comes to us in the word "anyone." It is Paul's way of saying what John wrote, "God so loved the world" (John 3:16). All three verses were ones I discovered and claimed as a new Christian.

It is a message for us all. Like iron filings are drawn to a magnet, we are all drawn to God. We are drawn as naturally as a deer is attracted to water (Psalm 42:1). Everyone is invited. No one is turned away.

Prayer: God, my faith in you is as natural as breathing, eating, and drinking. I am included in your amazing grace. Everyone is! Amen.

Week Seven, Day 3

Read 2 Corinthians 5:17-19

Everyone is made and meant to live "in Christ." This is the essence of Christian faith—life in Christ.[8] It is a metaphorical description rich with transforming and enriching features. But it is also a two-word witness to a genuine Holy Spirit/human spirit relationship.

Jesus interpreted the relationship in John 15. He used the relationship between a vine and a branch to describe it. He reveals life in him as a natural, continuous, fruitful, and joyful connection. Most of all, Jesus said, it is a relationship of love—for God and for one another.

Living "in Christ" is the most fulfilling life we can know. We are not absorbed in the relationship; we are activated by it. We live "in Christ" as those have united themselves to and found the life we long for.

Prayer: God, I connect myself to Christ, and doing so, I live. Amen.

Week Seven, Day 4

Read 2 Corinthians 5:17-19

By describing our life in Christ as a new creation, Paul was saying it is a life akin to the first creation. Our new life is of God (divine source), comprehensive (pertaining to all aspects of life), unique (not cloned), marvelously varied (not one-size-fits-all), and successively developed (little by little maturation).

Everyone and everything are of sacred worth, for God made all things. The new creation is, in fact, a fulfillment of the original creation. Spirituality is creation/new-creation life. The Celtic and Franciscan traditions especially instruct us in this way of living.

This life is interconnected and interdependent. We do not live by or unto ourselves. Life in Christ is essential oneness (Galatians 3:24 and Colossians 3:11). When we become new creations, we see that life is always life together.

Prayer: God, make me a new creation, bringing me out of individualism and into communion with everyone and everything. Amen.

Week Seven, Day 5

Read 2 Corinthians 5:17-19

The old has to go if the new is to come. We say it this way, "You can't have your cake and eat it to." Real change is not accommodation, it is transformation. Jesus made it clear: new wine must be poured into new wineskins (Mark 2:22).

What is the old? Paul did not make a list. But by looking at the context of this verse, we can deduce some things that have to pass away: thinking less of others than we do ourselves (Mark 2:16) and using that sense of superiority to separate ourselves from others.[9]

Jesus called this incomplete love. It is putting ourselves at the center, and then deciding who will and who will not be given love. This must pass away in all the ways it raises its ugly head in legalism, judgmentalism, supremacy, and sectarianism.

Prayer: God, take off of the shelf of my life anything that diminishes my love for you and for others. Amen.

Week Eight, Day 1

Read 2 Corinthians 5:17-19

We cannot move from the old to the new without there being a "passing away." Richard Rohr, in his *Falling Upward*, refers to this as necessary suffering.[10] In another place Paul described it as labor pains (Galatians 4:19). I put it this way: we have to slaughter our sacred cows.

There is nothing we resist more than change, and especially when the change means dethroning our ego and the support systems we have relied upon to remain in control. But egotism and the maintenance of power are the false self Jesus said we must deny if we are to follow him (Luke 9:23).

The "passing away" is essentially the transfer of trust from ourselves to God. It is coming to the place where we say, "You're God, I'm not."

Prayer: God, you've got me. Amen.

Week Eight, Day 2

Read 2 Corinthians 5:17-19

When we live on Christ, the new comes. Paul does not tell us what "new" means because it is not a limited list. *Christ* is the Christian word for everything. To live in Christ is to make all things in our life new.

We can see this newness in some areas of our life quickly. But for the rest, we are made new over time, step-by-step, little by little. That's why we do not define the Christian life by any single experience. Each step is a move into more Life. The "new" is a video not a photo.

Saint Francis is said to have started each day facing the rising sun, raising his arms, and saying, "Today, I begin with God." This is the spirit of abundant living, the attitude that keeps the "new" coming.

Prayer: God, I open myself to your unending newness. Amen.

Week Eight, Day 3

Read 2 Corinthians 5:17-19

Paul says, "All of these new things are from God." God is the giver. This is an important reminder. It is an essential check on our ego. This phrase reminds us that as the new comes, we give God the glory.

Jesus said we cannot do anything apart from him (John 15:5). He was not ignoring our strengths; he was pointing to their source. Dr. Dennis Kinlaw wrote similarly, reminding us that we are not self-generated, self-sustaining, or self-fulfilling.[11] We exist in a complex matrix of interdependent creation, all of which is God-made (John 1:3).

The most beautiful life comes from those who shine brightly without ever thinking they're the sun. About our total life we say, "All this comes from God."

Prayer: God, you are my maker, in everything. Amen.

Week Eight, Day 4

Read 2 Corinthians 5:17-19

Our new life in Christ reconciles us to God. Like iron filings are drawn toward a magnet, God restores us so that we are drawn to God. The action produces the purpose God had all along—to make us one with God.

But notice, the word to define the reconciliation is *us*, not *me*. God is at work in Christ to "bring all things together in Christ" (Ephesians 1:10). The magnet does not move one iron filing; it moves them all.

Salvation means wholeness, but it is not an individualized thing. It is universal. God is not "wanting anyone to perish" (2 Peter 3:9). God is "reconciling the world to himself" (2 Corinthians 5:19) in Christ. The outcome is a new creation—a new heaven and a new earth.

Prayer: God, help me understand that salvation is a "we" word, not a "me" word. Amen.

Week Eight, Day 5

Read 2 Corinthians 5:17-18

Christ has given us a ministry, the ministry of reconciliation. In a nutshell this means that what God wants for us is what God wants for everyone . . . and we are the ones to tell the world this is so.

We too often make evangelism a tedious task. But it is really introducing others to our best friend or spouse. We do not hesitate to say to another person, "There's someone I want you to know." We find great joy in doing this.

We have been reconciled to God by Christ. Reconciled people want everyone else to be reconciled to God. Our first step is to be reconciled to people ourselves, so there are no "others." We are one in Christ (Galatians 3:28). It is our ministry to act like it and work to make it so.

Prayer: God give me a heart to want everyone to experience in you what I experience in you. Amen.

Week Nine, Day 1

Read Mark 12:17

This story is often used to allege that Christians should stay out of politics. But a close reading of the text does not support that. On the contrary, Jesus says, "Give to Caesar what belongs to Caesar." The immediate thing to give was money, taxes, symbolized by the coin Jesus held in his hand.

But the coin also pointed to a legitimate loyalty to the state, including involvement in politics. The only thing Jesus prohibited was giving to Caesar what belonged to God—that is, ultimate allegiance. The state was never to be confused with the kingdom of God. Christians were meant to be good citizens but not intended to glorify the system or any leader in it.

In my lifetime, some Christians have blended their faith and politics into a religious nationalism that is toxic. Citizenship has become an expression of idolatry. This must not be so for you, and it must not remain so for the nation.

Prayer: God, I give you my ultimate allegiance. Nothing and no one else. Amen.

Week Nine, Day 2

Read Psalm 100

The spiritual life cannot be reduced to a formula. But it can be described in principles. One foundational principle is this: grace + response = growth. We see this principle throughout the Bible. Psalm 100 is a good place to explore it.

This psalm moves toward the main point: God is good, a goodness defined as "loyal love" ("steadfast love" in other translations)—God's never-ending, never-give-up-on-us love. That's the revelation, coming in verse 5. Our response is on verses 1-4, summarized in two words: *worship* and *service*, which are the summation of the two great commandments. Making this response to revelation, we grow in our love of God and others.

The spiritual life is our recognition that we are God-created, not self-made. In this psalm we are called sheep; that is, people willing to follow the good God, who leads us more into the life of love.

Prayer: God, guide me along the path that increases my love for you, and for others. Fill my life with love until my cup runs over. Amen.

Week Nine, Day 3

Read Colossians 3:11

E. Stanley Jones called this verse the most important sentence ever written.[12] It flattens every hierarchical system, dethroning supremacy. It fosters community, enthroning equality. The gospel removes walls that divide, replacing them with bridges that connect.

The ultimate peril today is partisanship that creates systems to promote and preserve it. We are drowning in a sea of separations. Our future is at stake.

Christ is the sign that God is at work to get life back on track. *Christ* is the Christian word for ultimacy ("Christ is all") and for universality ("Christ is in all"). This is not just the Christian message, it is one for "all." God is calling us to be instruments of peace, of shalom—comprehensive well-being. We are invited to be co-laborers with God in the creation of Beloved Community.

Prayer: God, give me eyes to see your vision of life in all and for all, and the will to work for it. Amen.

Week Nine, Day 4

Read Ephesians 4:15

We sometimes refer to the spiritual life as a "balanced life." If we think of balance as equilibrium, the idea is confusing. We are rarely "in balance." In fact, we are only in balance in our walk when we are standing still. Walking requires imbalance.

But a balanced spiritual life makes sense when we think of it as a balanced diet, eating from all the food groups. That kind of balance is nutritious and life-giving.

In the spiritual life six historic "food groups" keep us strong and healthy: the contemplative tradition, the holiness tradition, the social justice tradition, the charismatic tradition, the evangelical tradition, and the incarnational tradition.[13] The nutrients they provide create the balanced spiritual life.

Prayer: God, I want to eat well so I can live well. Amen.

Week Nine, Day 5

Read Psalm 119:105

In ancient Israel people walked at night carrying small oil lamps in their hands. The lamps illuminated only the next step or two, but that was enough to keep going. Similarly, we cannot see the whole of our faith journey. We travel with lamps, not halogen lights. We usually see only a step or two ahead.

Amy Carmichael wrote of this kind of spiritual walk, "if only the next step is clear, then the one thing to do is take it."[14] She had to do this for decades after an accident increasingly rendered her less mobile. But she never stopped walking.

We can walk a million miles one step at a time. In fact, that's how we walk all the time, even when we can see for miles. God is our light, often only an oil lamp's worth. But with even that much light, we can make it every step of the way.

Prayer: God, you are my light. I walk with you step by step. Amen.

❦

Week Ten, Day 1

Read Acts 4:13

There is no finer witness for us to make than for others to see that we have been with Jesus. But how can people tell this? The verse offers two clues. First, the apostles lived confidently. And second, they evidenced wisdom beyond their education. Both of these qualities came from the time they had spent with Jesus.

That's where our witness comes from. It comes from our relationship with Christ. Like the first apostles it may include confidence and wisdom. But at the core, the authenticity is Christlike—it looks and sounds like Jesus.

The church has summarized Christlikeness in the fruit of the Spirit (Galatians 5:22-23). People can tell we have been with Jesus when we are loving, joyful, peaceful, patient, kind, good, faithful, gentle, and self-controlled. This is so important that upcoming meditations will explore each of these aspects of life.

Prayer: God, I want to live so that others can tell I have been with Jesus. Amen.

Week Ten, Day 2

Read Galatians 5:22-23

Have you noticed that Paul says the fruit of the Spirit "is" and then names nine things? Why did he not use the plural verb "are"? Most likely because there is a oneness that holds the nine qualities together.

If we let Paul speak for himself, he almost certainly would say the singularity is love, the greatest of all the virtues (1 Corinthians 13:13). John Wesley felt the same, calling love "the root of all the rest."[15]

The life of love is the life of God (who is love) in the human soul, life that expresses itself (inwardly and outwardly) in the other eight ways—and more. When love is alive in us, everything else follows. In upcoming posts the next eight qualities will be viewed as expressions of love.

Prayer: God, I seek you. I seek love—to be love and to do love. Amen.

Week Ten, Day 3

Read Galatians 5:22-23

Joy is love celebrating. Sometimes it is celebration because of something that has happened. But the kind of joy Paul is describing does not rise and fall with our circumstances.

Joy is also celebrating with confidence that God is present and active in our lives all the time. We are never alone, never abandoned (Psalm 23:4). This is Emmanuel, God with us.

Julian of Norwich is remembered for her joy in the midst of a pandemic. She summed up hopeful joy in these words, "All shall be well, and all manner of things shall be well." We too can know joy when we live in challenging times.

Prayer: God my joy is in you, and you are always with me. Amen.

Week Ten, Day 4

Read Galatians 5:22-23

Peace is love's wellness. It includes things like the cessation of war and the taming of conflict. But it expands beyond such things to mean that our whole life is in good working order. The biblical word for it is *shalom*.

We drive down the road in peace when all the parts of our automobile are functioning properly. Similarly, we travel the road of life in peace when all facets of our existence are in sync.

Peace is comprehensive well-being because the Holy Spirit is at work for good in all areas of our life (Philippians 2:13). Nothing is big enough to keep God out. Nothing is small enough to be insignificant. From top to bottom, and inside out, God is present and active. That's peace.

Prayer: God, I am all yours. Amen.

Week Ten, Day 5

Read Galatians 5:22-23

Patience is love enduring. People who change things understand that change occurs little by little. "Quick fixes" may look good, but they don't fix much. Lasting change is a long-haul endeavor.

If anyone knew this, it was Jesus. His message was the coming of the kingdom of God. But he knew it emerges more like a sunrise than a lightning bolt. Even after three years with his disciples, the whole enterprise was fragile.

Patience is the fruit of the Spirit that not only recognizes the incrementality of change, it also accepts the inevitability of opposition. Those who live in darkness, Jesus said, resist the light (John

3:19). Patience is slow-going confidence in the rightness of what we are about, and the willingness to measure success inch by inch.

Prayer: God, this little light of mine, I'm gonna let it shine, as long as it takes. Amen.

⤜⤝

Week Eleven, Day 1

Read Galatians 5:22-23

Kindness is love's compassion. It is the Spirit-inspired choice to live benevolently. Kindness is living for the sake of others.

Jesus is said to have responded to individuals and groups with compassion. He allowed their situation to enter his heart, and he entered their situation with his heart. Compassion inspired his action. Jesus's kindness moved people from where they were to where they needed to be.

Kindness is the sign that we are noticing other people and taking them seriously. Kindness is saying to others, "Your life matters. Your story matters."[16] Kindness is in play when people know we care by how we treat them. Kindness is caring beyond words.

Prayer: God, give me a compassionate heart that is manifested in a helping hand. Amen.

Week Eleven, Day 2

Read Galatians 5:22-23

Goodness is love's character. Of course, it is an action, but it is an action born from a deeper virtue. Solomon described this long ago, "Guard your heart, for everything you do flows from it"

(Proverbs 4:23 NIV). What's happening on the outside of us is the indicator of what's inside us.

We are often told, "Do the right thing," and that is good advice. But the reality and realization of the counsel comes from a deeper wisdom, "Be the right person." Ethics is not a choice as much as it is a condition.

We are not talking about the bare minimum. The idea of goodness is one of generosity, goodness to the max. Spirit-inspired goodness does not ask, "What's the least I can do?" It seeks the highest good . . . for all.

Jesus went about doing good because he was good—in every way and to the greatest extent. His conduct flowed from his character. Ours does too.

Prayer: "Create in me a clean heart, O God, and put a new and right spirit within me" (Psalm 51:10 NRSVue). Amen.

Week Eleven, Day 3

Read Galatians 5:22-23

Faithfulness is love's trustworthiness. Faithfulness describes a person who is dependable. It's what we mean when we say, "You can count on him or her." It is a quality that makes others secure and confident in our presence.

This is why infidelity in any area of life is so devastating. It destroys the foundation for life together. Faithfulness, on the other hand, is the steel cord running through life that can hold us together when other things are strained or missing (e.g., understanding, agreement). As long as we can say, "I trust you," we can hang in there with each other.

Motives are the sinews of solidarity. Faithfulness means that even when we get it wrong, we are trying to get it right. Faithfulness keeps the conversation going, and as long as we can talk to one another, there is hope that we can live with one another.

Prayer: God work on my life so people will always know they can count on me. Amen.

Week Eleven, Day 4

Read Galatians 5:22-23

Gentleness is love's humility, the quality of blessedness Jesus commended in Matthew 5:5. It is life that is inwardly teachable and outwardly respectful. Some call this being tender, the opposite of being harsh.

It is easy to be too hard on ourselves and on others, a hardness driven by perfectionism, so that neither we nor others ever "measure up." We feel inwardly guilty and outwardly critical. We become bitter.

Gentleness is a tenderness that "travels lightly." It does not carry excess baggage or impose heavy burdens. It does not condemn. Gentleness creates spaciousness inwardly and outwardly, so that life flourishes. Gentleness is the perception that God is not finished with any of us. So, gentleness is life that never gives up. We are all subject to change.

Prayer: God, you never give up on anyone. Neither will I, beginning with myself and extending to everyone else. Amen.

Week Eleven, Day 5

Read Galatians 5:22-23

Self-control is love's restraint. It is the opposite of egotism and ethnocentrism. It is, as Paul described it, love that "doesn't seek its own advantage" (1 Corinthians 13:5).

Sadly, we live in a narcissistic (individual) and partisan (collective) age. We see how the whole idea of Christlikeness (the fruit of the Spirit) can "die on the vine" when self-control is absent. Nothing destroys the life of God in the human soul more than a "my way or the highway" attitude.

Self-control acknowledges the fullness of our human potential. But it teaches us that this potential is realized when we live for the sake of others. Paul's list of the fruit of the Spirit ends in what we call the Golden Rule, "Do unto others as you would have them do unto you." That's self-control.

Prayer: God, save me from selfishness. Amen.

❦

Week Twelve, Day 1

Read Acts 2:17-21

Pentecost was the means God used to make clear that the fruit of the Spirit that we have looked at was meant for the world. Pentecost was God's way of saying, "Everyone is included in the outpouring of the Holy Spirit." It took a while for this to sink in to the early church. The idea of radical, universal inclusion has been, and still is, a difficult thing to accept and to implement. But it is the will of God.

Peter began his Pentecost day sermon declaring that what was happening was not new, not a flash in the pan, not an aberration. It was a fulfillment of prophecy in the Old Testament (Joel 2:28-32). By starting here, Peter was saying that Pentecost was the act of God in Israel to restore the land (indeed, the world) to the way God intended it to be. Looking at the larger passage in Joel (2:18-32), we see Pentecost was a healing. In the next round of meditations, we will look at inclusion as the means to that healing.

Prayer: Seeing you in everyone, I see you the way you mean to be seen. Amen.

Week Twelve, Day 2

Read Acts 2:17 and 3:25

Pentecost was a healing of the covenant. Given in three stages to Noah (Genesis 9:1-17), Abraham (Genesis 17), and to Moses (Deuteronomy 10), God clearly showed that the covenant was for all living beings. The Israelites were the focal point, not as possessors of the covenant, but as proclaimers of it. The message is universality.[17]

Over time, the universality of the covenant was eclipsed by exclusivism, creating the false impression that the Jews as the "chosen people" were superior to others when, in fact, they were "chosen" by God to be servants telling everyone else they are God's beloved.

Pentecost healed partiality and exclusion, restoring the "all flesh" reality God had intended the covenant to define and create. Inclusion is the sign that we are living the covenant.

Prayer: God, I want to be a covenant person, including "all flesh" in the Story of your love and in the expression of my love. Amen.

Week Twelve, Day 3

Read Acts 2:17

Pentecost was a healing of genders. The foundational equality of gender in the *imago Dei* (Genesis 1:26-27) had become a hierarchy of male superiority. What was actually a result of the fall (Genesis 3:16) had been made to appear the divine order.

Pentecost reordered the disorder. In the new covenant, in the age of the Spirit, sons and daughters would prophesy—that is, be fully and equally involved in living and sharing God's Story. Before the close of the New Testament, we see women engaged in all five offices of ministry: apostles (Romans 16:7), prophets (1 Corinthians 11:5), evangelists (Acts 9:21), pastors (1 Timothy 3:10), and teachers (Acts 18:26; Titus 2:3).

Pentecost healed gender hierarchy, engaging sons and daughters in Christian life and ministry. Inclusion is the sign that we are living in the *imago Dei*.

Prayer: God, I claim my equality and I respect it in everyone else. Amen.

Week Twelve, Day 4

Read Acts 2:17

Pentecost was a healing of the generations. Young and old participate in God's Story, with each holding a key facet of it.

The young see visions. They keep the energy of renewal alive. They prevent us from turning the status quo into a sacred cow. They are the envisioners for whom change and "new and improved" life is attractive.

The old dream dreams. They keep the treasures of the past alive in the present. They prevent us from embracing novelty as an end, but rather help us see the present in the sacred flow of past, present, and future. They are the encouragers who have learned by experience that failure is not final and life goes on.

Pentecost healed partiality, recreating the whole Story that we see when young and old show and tell their part of it.

Prayer: God, I take my age and stage of life and connect it with those younger and older than I am, so that we can know, show, and tell your whole Story. Amen.

Week Twelve, Day 5

Read Acts 2:18

Pentecost was a healing of social distinctions. Servants (both men and women) would prophesy along with everyone else. The outpouring of the Holy Spirit was the sign that all people are on equal footing.

Jesus bore witness to this in his ministry, making servanthood the definition of greatness (Matthew 23:11). Our worth as human beings is not determined by our status, but by our servanthood. Pentecost confirmed what Jesus said.

We find numerous ways to establish "have" and "have not" distinctions. But they are all artificial in the sight of God. God looks at us and sees one thing: human being. God looks at us together and sees one thing: human family. When the Spirit comes upon us, we see people this way too.

Prayer: God, give me the singular vision that you have. Amen.

❧❧

Week Thirteen, Day 1

Read: Acts 2:19-20

Pentecost was a healing of the earth. The word *salvation* means wholeness, not going to heaven when we die. Because God created the cosmos, the heavens and the earth, it stands to reason that God would heal all of nature, not just human nature.

Paul made it plain that the earth was fallen, like everyone and everything else (Romans 8:22). But he adds, "until now"—the now of Pentecost, the time of the outpouring of the Spirit (Romans 8:23). The images from Joel are vivid, but they all point to the redemption of the natural order.

The Bible never separates reality into disparate pieces. Life is one. God is at work to heal people and things, from the tiniest particle to the farthest star. Pentecost was a sign that the whole world is in God's hand.

Prayer: God, you have a heart for the world. Give me that same heart. Amen.

Week Thirteen, Day 2

Read Acts 2:21

Pentecost was a healing of limitation. It reissued the message "Salvation is for all." We are not told precisely what it means to call on the name of the Lord, and we must be careful not to read something into the text that's not there.

But something is there, the word *everyone*. Every notion of partiality disappeared at Pentecost. The message (which was true all along, but got lost over time) is universality. This is another confirmation of the "all people" message in 2:17.

Universality is the overarching message of Pentecost. All nations (2:5). All genders (2:17). All ages (2:17). All classes (2:18). All creation (2:29-20). All means all.

Prayer: God, give me life in the Spirit, where there are no walls, no barriers, and no limits—where all "in/out" thinking is eliminated. Amen.

Week Thirteen, Day 3

Read Galatians 3:28

The message of Pentecost became the mission of the church. The book of Acts shows how the first Christians enacted the message in Jerusalem, Judea, Samaria, and to the ends of the earth (Acts 1:8).

Paul's words in today's text sum it up, using the same categories as Pentecost to describe the inclusion restored by the Spirit, and going beyond them to declare, "you are all one in Christ Jesus." The rest of the New Testament reveals how this radical inclusion took root in the early church, and church history has continued to tell the story as Christianity has moved down the corridors of time and into our time.

The story moves beyond our day to the end of time as we know it, when God will bring the Pentecostal message to fulfillment, bringing "all things together in Christ" (Ephesians 1:10). We are the heirs of the Pentecostal reality, and we are meant to be the witnesses of it.

Prayer: God, I am who I am because of the Spirit's work in me. I offer myself to you as a means through whom to tell this Story to others. Amen.

Week Thirteen, Day 4

Read Acts 2:37-38

The outpouring of the Spirit produced immediate and long-lasting fruit (Galatians 5:22-23).[18] But it did not happen accidentally or automatically. It happened through the responsiveness of the people to what was going on. Peter summed up that responsiveness in two ways: repentance and baptism.

Repentance meant people were willing to look at life in a new way—the way of Christ. Baptism meant people were willing to identify with Christ's way and commit themselves to personifying it.

The process is the same for us. We too must see life in a new way (i.e., as life in the Spirit) and devote ourselves to embracing and enacting that life. Otherwise, Pentecost deteriorates into a topic when it was meant to be a transformation.

Prayer: God, I see and accept your way. Amen.

Week Thirteen, Day 5

Read Acts 10:34-35

It took a while for the message of Pentecost to sink in to the Christian community. But little by little (beginning in 8:1) the Spirit confirmed the universality of Pentecost, culminating with Peter's individual experience in today's reading and with the church's collective decision in Acts 15.

Old ways do not pass away quickly. Ice melts slowly. The Holy Spirit shines like the sun, warming our hearts with the realization that everyone is loved by God and included in the restoration of all things in Christ (Ephesians 2:9-10).

Pentecost was the initial splash of God's rock falling into the water of the world in Jerusalem. But like every splash, it created a ripple effect that reaches downward to the smallest particle and outward to the farthest star. One of those ripples reached the shoreline of your life, making Peter's words real for you right where you are.

Prayer: God, I feel your wave of grace washing over me. Thank you. Amen.

Week Fourteen, Day 1

Read Lamentations 3:22-23

The hymn "Great Is Thy Faithfulness" is based on this reading in Lamentations. It is the Bible's revelation set to music: God is with us when we hit rock bottom. Israel had done this in spades. In every way imaginable Israel was at the bottom of the barrel. But God's faithful love and compassion was there too.

God's faithfulness does not ignore the past. The verses that precede and follow the ones in today's reading make that clear. Neither does God's faithfulness change the past. What's done is done.

God does not erase our memory; God heals our memory. How? By not allowing the past to control our present or determine our future. God's healing grace (faithful love and compassion) is renewed every morning. God's ultimate word to us is this: you can always make a fresh start.

Prayer: God, I acknowledge the past, but I refuse to live in. I accept your love and receive your compassion to live a new life in whatever ways I need to do so. Amen.

Week Fourteen, Day 2

Read: Luke 6:38

Much of the Christian life is paradoxical. It goes against the grain of conventional thinking. The idea of having is one such thing. The usual notion is that having is getting. This makes having about accumulation, taking in, and so on. It turns having into a quantity. More is better.

Jesus turned the idea upside down, saying that we receive by giving. Having is not a quantity, it's a quality. For Jesus, having is the return of joy on the investment of our resources for the sake of others. Less is more.

Jesus's words transform life from a consumption mentality to a consecration mindset. Our life is elevated when others are enriched. We thrive when we have a "what's mine is yours, I'll share it" heart—a disposition that comes back to us with joy that's packed down, firmly shaken, and overflowing.

Prayer: God, give me a spirit of stewardship. Amen.

Week Fourteen, Day 3

Read 1 Thessalonians 5:18

Gratitude is meant to be a foundational disposition of our heart "in every situation." But it's these three words that make gratitude a struggle. Some things happen that should never have happened—things that are undeserved, unfair, and unjust—that bring great suffering to us and to others.

Paul knew about this kind of suffering (2 Corinthians 1:8-11), and yet he exhorted the Thessalonians to be thankful in all circumstances. What kind of gratitude is this? It is gratefulness not based on our circumstances, but in our confidence that God is with us in everything.

Of course, there are times when our gratitude arises from our blessings. But it is not limited to those times. Gratitude is ultimately our response to the fact that we are never alone.

Prayer: God, I thank you for your abiding presence in my life, no matter what. Amen.

Week Fourteen, Day 4

Read Matthew 7:7

It's been said that prayer is to the spiritual life what experimentation is to science. That's the spirit of Jesus's invitation to ask, seek, and knock. All three words are experiments. All three acts make us explorers.

Asking is Jesus's invitation to inquire—to bring our questions to the table. Questions are not a sign of weak faith; they are indications of faith wanting to grow stronger. Seeking is the drilling phase, taking what has gotten our attention and looking at it in more detail—mining our discoveries for all they're worth. Knocking is entering into a living experience with what we have found. It is moving inside the house, living now as a resident, not just a researcher.

Asking, seeking, and knocking are expressions of prayer, experiments in response to the Spirit's promptings. They take the grand revelations of God and bring them to life in us. In asking, we receive. In seeking, we find. In knocking, doors are opened. We experience living faith.

Prayer: God, sign me up to be part of your exploratory expedition. Amen.

Week Fourteen, Day 5

Read Romans 14:19

We are called to live for the common good, looking not only to our interests but also to the interests of others (Philippians 2:4). The Bible only understands life as life together.

The originating sin (egotism and ethnocentrism) defines life selfishly. The manner of distorted living is narcissism; it has two mantras, "What's mine is mine, I'll keep it." and "What's yours is mine, I'll take it." Most of the problems we face stem from these roots.

God redeems us from this outlook, restoring the reality of mutual edification on which we say, "What's mine is yours, I'll share it." Jesus called it becoming a servant, and he went on to say that servanthood is what defines the truly great life (Matthew 23:11). Such a life is not an obligation; it is an opportunity for "encouraging each other and building each other up" (1 Thessalonians 5:11). It is the life that brings us great joy.

Prayer: God, give me eyes to see beyond myself, and a heart for doing good to those I see. Amen.

Week Fifteen, Day 1

Read Psalm 130

Some people keep track of their sins so much that they come to the conclusion "God could never forgive me." And even if they think God is able to forgive, their pile of sins convinces them God is unwilling to do so.

That's the exact opposite of what this psalm says. Instead of what we mistakenly think, it tells us what God thinks: God does not keep track of our sins (v. 3); God forgives all of them (v. 8). There is no sin God refuses to forgive; there is no mountain of sin too high for God to climb and plant the flag of forgiveness at the top of it.

In the Eucharist, the officiant says without qualification or limit, "In the name of Jesus Christ, you are forgiven." And we respond, reminding the officiant, "In the name of Jesus Christ, you are forgiven." It's a clean sweep, to which we all then say, "Thanks be to God." Thanks be to God, indeed!

Prayer: God, I bring my sins to you, confessing them in confidence that you forgive them all. Amen.

Week Fifteen, Day 2

Read Leviticus 19:11

The Bible forbids lying. Telling lies is bad enough, but there is something worse: becoming a lie—that is, becoming a person whose life is essentially a testimony to falsehood. It is possible to tell lies so often and for so long that we become strangers to the truth. We no longer recognize truth, and even if we do, we have no interest in promoting it.

There is no sadder life than the one that is built and sustained by lies. There is no more broken person than one whose identity is shaped by lying. This is the apex of the false self. To sink to that level is to lose all self-respect and all respect for others. To become a lying person is to cease to love. It shatters the love of God, others, and self. It is the maximum manifestation of brokenness.

Jesus was truth incarnate (John 14:6), and he calls us to know the truth (the Greek means to know experientially—that is, to live the truth, to be truthful people. He said this is the life that sets us free (John 8:32).

Prayer: God, make me truth full. Amen.

Week Fifteen, Day 3

Read Romans 5:1-5

When we ask ourselves how things are going, we usually find we are doing OK in some areas, but not so well in others. Our lives are a mixture of positives and negatives, and some neutrals too.

When we think of spiritual growth, we easily think of it in terms of accentuating the positive. But Paul writes that growth occurs both in our possibilities and our problems, in our strengths and weakness. To strengthen his point, he says we can take pride in our problems. They teach us too.

This is the concept that God works through everything in our lives. Of course, we prefer good times to bad times, but God is not present in the good and absent in the bad. God's grace is with us in everything. We can learn from every circumstance and grow in every situation.

Prayer: God, thank you for being with me in everything. Amen.

Week Fifteen, Day 4

Read John 15:15

We do not mind calling ourselves servants of Christ. But Jesus made it clear that our relationship with him is more than that. To him, we are not his servants, we are his friends. Friendship is what Jesus has in mind for us. He wants to be our friend, and he wants us to be his.

Servants are never in the inner circle, but friends are. Today's reading tells us so. Servants are told what to do, and they do it; it's all regulated. But Jesus did not ask us to follow orders; he invited us to follow him. Servants are hirelings, friends are colleagues. Most of all, servants come and go, but friends are friends forever. That is the only kind of relationship Jesus wants to have with us.

Our discipleship anthem is "What a Friend We Have in Jesus." And as the song says, "What a privilege it is to carry everything to God in prayer." Everything. When we understand that we are Jesus's friends, discipleship is transformed from being a duty into being a delight. Friendship is not an obligation, it's an opportunity.

Prayer: God, thank you for sending Jesus to let us know that you want us to be your friends, not your employees. Amen.

Week Fifteen, Day 5

Read Joshua 1:5-6

When we were children, there were times when we were afraid to go into new places. We would turn to our parents and say, "I'll go if you'll go with me." We derived our courage from another's presence.

Interestingly, God's presence was the basis for Joshua's courage. "I'll be with you," God said, "so be strong and courageous." God took the initiative to tell Joshua, "You can have the courage to succeed Moses and carry on this formidable task because I am accompanying you."

God's promise was not a sign of Joshua's cowardice, but rather an indication that Joshua was wise, knowing that the source of his strength and success was not in himself but in God. In other words, Joshua's courage was not bravado, it was belief—his belief that he would never face his perils alone. God's companionship is the foundation and force for our courage.

Prayer: God, I will go, because I know you are with me. Amen.

Week Sixteen, Day 1

Read Jeremiah 6:13-16

Trading in dishonesty is bad (v. 13); doing it with no shame is worse (v. 15). But that's how far down Jeremiah found the nation.

God sent him to be a prophet, calling out sin and calling forth hope, in a time when shameless dishonesty prevailed.

God sends us to do the same when nations default on their purpose to promote the common good and engage in exclusionary evil. Life is never as God intends when it arises out of the absence of conscience.

But how do we speak and act as those through whom God works to restore righteousness? Jeremiah provides an answer: we look for the ancient paths and seek the good way (v. 16). There are many ways to do this, but keeping our vows (ancient paths) and listening to our wisest voices (good way) are two primary means. In this respect we have vowed in baptism to resist evil, and our finest guides tell us to do that by manifesting the fruit of the Spirit (Galatians 5:22-23). We must be courageous, living nonviolently to overcome evil with good.

Prayer: God, I promise to keep my deepest vows and listen to our wisest voices. Amen.

Week Sixteen, Day 2

Read Luke 18:21

These words of Jesus are often used to support "heart religion"—that is, the priority of the inner life, the source from which our outer life emerges and expresses itself. There's no doubt that this is part of what he meant.

But it is likely not all he meant, given that he spoke the words in a period of upheaval in Israel. To say the kingdom is within was to say two other things. First, the kingdom is not in the imperialism all around formed by the political/religious collusion people saw every day. And second, Jesus said that the kingdom is not elsewhere or delayed in an eternity where everything is made right.

He was saying that the kingdom of God is not in the world ("the system") or in heaven ("the sweet by-and-by"). It is here and now, alive and active "within you"—in people who live in the present moment by the principles and power of the indwelling Spirit. In these three meanings, Jesus set forth the most counter-cultural message possible, then and now.

Prayer: God, I look within to find and form my life without. And what I find, I will live here and now in the Spirit. Amen.

Week Sixteen, Day 3

Read Matthew 18:1-5

We often read Jesus's words and begin compiling a list of commendable childhood qualities. And that's OK. Jesus commended the humility of children, and they surely have other characteristics akin to life in the kingdom of God.

But Jesus was also making a social statement. Children had no social standing, no status. They were not climbing any ladders or offering any perks. Their value lay in who they were—blessed ones.

Becoming like a child means refusing to define ourselves by conventional standards (e.g., prestige, power, productivity, possessions), and instead looking to our personhood. Our being, not our doing and having, is where we find our value, and is where we turn to discern the characteristics of kingdom living.

Prayer: God, thank you for placing my sacred worth in my personhood, not my performance. Amen.

Week Sixteen, Day 4

Read Psalm 139:14

This psalm tells us two things about ourselves. It says we are reverently ("fearfully," KJV) made. We are people of inestimable worth. The psalm then says we are marvelously ("wonderfully," KJV) made. We are unique and unrepeatable.

Taken together, these verses tell us we are sacredly specific. God does not see us as indistinguishable waves in the sea of humanity. Instead, we are named individually, forever known and loved by God (Isaiah 49:16; John 10:14).

From this verse we glean two additional truths. We must never seek our value by trying to be like someone else. Instead, God says, "Be who you are." And we must never label people, stereotype, or caricature them. Instead, God says, "Get to know people rather than judging them from afar."

Prayer: God, thank you for making me who I am, and for making others as they are. You are OK with both things. I will be too. Amen.

Week Sixteen, Day 5

Read Psalm 27:10

Many people did not grow up in good homes. Some only remember either abandonment or abuse, or both. When this is the case, it is easy to think God has rejected us too.

David said otherwise in this psalm. God takes us in when others throw us out. God never abandons or forgets us (Isaiah 49:16). God is with us always (Matthew 28:20).

People who are victimized naturally ask, "Where was God when bad things were happening to me?" On one level this is an unanswerable question, and we all wonder why God did not step in to stop evil. It is a mystery.

But what is not a mystery is this: in the worst moments of our lives, God was and is with us. Immanuel—"God is with us." God is with us in our darkest valleys (Psalm 23:4). God is our refuge and strength in times of trouble (Psalm 46:1). Knowing this, we find grace to carry on and even to restore what others should never have taken from us.

Prayer: God, you return to me the years the locusts have eaten (Joel 2:25). Your presence with me assures me there are no dead ends, only new beginnings. Amen.

Week Seventeen, Day 1

Read Psalm 23

We tend to live like the God we believe in. If our concept of God is wrong, it has a negative effect on everything else. If it is right, every aspect of our life is positively influenced.

David called the Lord his shepherd. Having been a shepherd himself, it was his way of complimenting God and telling others God is good. But it was more—"shepherd" is a name God used for self-disclosure. God relates to us as a shepherd does to sheep.

More than any other passage of scripture, people have memorized this one to remind themselves, "This is who God is." The Twenty-Third Psalm is an art gallery, with a number of paintings hanging in it to reveal God's nature and to show us what God, our shepherd, does for us. This week we will stand before the paintings, gazing at them as a portrait of God, a God who has moved people for thousands of years to exclaim, "I can love a God like that!"

Prayer: God, as my shepherd, I gladly understand that I am your sheep. I heartily give myself to you. Amen.

Week Seventeen, Day 2

Read Psalm 23:2-3

As our shepherd, God goes ahead of us. In that position, God lets us rest, gives us peace, and guides us in our journey. Jesus, the Good Shepherd, located himself ahead of us when he said, "Follow me."

We end up where we are led. Followers become like their leaders. No one is self-made. We are shaped by our associations. Psalm 1 makes this clear. David made the same point here. The guidance of God gives us what we need: strength, well-being, and righteousness.

One of the most important questions we ever ask is "Whom am I following?" The fact is, we are always following someone. If our leaders are offering us life-giving qualities, we should continue to follow them. If not, we should look elsewhere.

Prayer: God, thank you for going ahead of me, offering me light, life, and love as you do so. Amen.

Week Seventeen, Day 3

Read Psalm 23:4

As our shepherd, God walks beside us. In that position God guides (the staff) and guards (the rod) us. Jesus, the Good Shepherd, located himself beside us when he said, "I am with you always."

We cannot read this verse without recognizing that God comes near to us in times of danger and darkness. When everything is going well, God can be "out there, somewhere." But when predators and valleys are our lot, a God-belief will not do. A perspective must become a presence, so God becomes a companion, not a concept.

God's nearness is a kind of leading—the kind we need when we cannot see where to go. God walks with us step-by-step, and God's little by little accompaniment gets us through.

Prayer: God, thank you for walking beside me, guarding me against my foes and guiding me through my fears. Amen.

Week Seventeen, Day 4

Read Psalm 23:5

As our shepherd, God provides for us. In God's provision there is nourishment (table and cup) and healing (oil). Jesus identified himself as our provider in both these ways—feeding us (as the Bread and Water of life) and healing us.

Provision is the sign that God takes our lives seriously. Shepherds prepared table lands where their sheep could graze. At the end of the day, shepherds put oil on their sheep's wounds and let them drink in big gulps. The shepherd was the caregiver of the sheep.

One of the great illusions is that we are self-made. But the truth is, none of us is self-sustaining. A complex food chain and water system keeps us nourished and an intricate immune system keeps us well. God provides for us by creating these natural support systems in us and for us, along with accompanying human systems to deliver life and health to us.

Prayer: God, thank you for caring for me, and through all your means of provision reminding me that my whole life matters to you. Amen.

Week Seventeen, Day 5

Read Psalm 23:6

As our shepherd, God is with us for the long haul. God is our sustainer, giving us goodness and faithful love all the days of our lives and giving us an eternal dwelling place. Jesus, the Good Shepherd, confirmed this by offering grace, and by promising to come for us and take us home.

This psalm holds time and eternity in a dynamic relationship that religion sometimes separates. What God wills for us is not for this world only. Nor is what God wills for us put off to some future time and place. Here and now moves into an eternity without skipping a beat, and as two expressions of a singular reality.

The portraits of God that hang in the gallery we call the Twenty-Third Psalm combine to create the even larger reality that life in God is one in which we "lack nothing" (v. 1). The life of God in the human soul is total grace for every need.

Prayer: God, it is true—in you I live, move, and have my being (Acts 17:28). Thank you! Amen.

❧

Week Eighteen, Day 1

Read Mark 10:46-52

"What do you want me to do for you?" (v. 51). It's an open-ended question—one that Jesus used to let people know he took their lives seriously, and that what was a concern of theirs was also a concern of his.

It's a question that shows he did not enter people's lives with a preconceived, one-size-fits-all formula. Rather, it was an indication that Jesus wanted to have genuine relationships with people, and in those relationships honor the sacredness of their specificity.

Imagine Jesus coming to your house, sitting with you, and asking, "What do you want me to do for you?" What would you say?

Prayer: God, thank you for caring enough about my life to act specifically in it. Amen.

Week Eighteen, Day 2

Read Genesis 1:5

We do not live by the natural cycles much anymore. Electric lights enable us to rise before sunrise and stay up after sunset. We can cross time zones in jet planes and really mess up our body clock.

But there are moments when we get in sync with nature's rhythms, and when we do, we feel both relaxed and refreshed. In the creation story, the day begins with evening—a reminder that God never slumbers or sleeps even when we do (Psalm 121:3). By beginning with evening the creation story tells us that resting and sleeping are not as much about recovering from work as they are preparing ourselves for it.

There are cultures around the world that stay more in tune with natural cycles, and those that do sense a kinship with the heavens and the earth. They are also far less taken with activism and more inclined to see nature as a provider than a product. Living in sync with nature, we trust and rest.

Prayer: God, thank you for those moments when I sense my oneness with all you have made. Help me live more in sync with your rhythms. Amen.

Week Eighteen, Day 3

Read Hebrews 11:1

Faith and trust are the signs of faith, not beliefs. But sadly, we have made beliefs litmus tests for what we say faith is, and is not. But at their best, beliefs are only the containers of faith, not the content of it.

Discover your convictions, not your creeds, if you want to find your faith. Name what you are hoping for and what you are trusting in, and you will declare your faith. Faith is what we value, not merely what we verbalize.

As the rest of Hebrews 11 shows, faith is what we are willing to live for and ready to die for. Faith is what we value most, not what we verbalize most often. History leaves a well-worn trail of tears walked by "people of faith" who said and did horrible things. It also reveals a path of righteousness walked by those who said little but loved much. Faith manifests our hopes and evidences our trust.

Prayer: God, you are the object of my faith, not words written about you. In you I hope. In you I trust. Amen.

Week Eighteen, Day 4

Read Matthew 5:17

Unfortunately, when we point to the inclusiveness of Jesus, some react and falsely allege that we make him one who did not care about the Law and the Prophets. But this is not what we are saying, and that's because he denied he was opposed to either of them.

What he said was that he came to fulfill them. The Greek word for "fulfill" means to restore the fullness in something that has been lost. Jesus was not antinomian, he was agape-oriented, and this section of the Sermon on the Mount moves from his words in 5:17 to his conclusion in 5:48 to make that clear.

The Law and the Prophets are filled full when love prevails—when we love everyone (not just those who love us or think well of us); when our love is complete (the meaning of "perfect"), not partial (5:43-48). The fact is, when we point to the inclusiveness of Jesus, we are only bearing witness to his words and works. When we declare his fulfillment of the Law and the Prophets in the word *love*, we are accepting his call to do likewise.

Prayer: God, make me to love as you love, and I will live in the confidence that love-life fulfills all the rest. Amen.

Week Eighteen, Day 5

Read Acts 11:19-26

Before Antioch, Jesus's disciples were called "persons who belonged to the Way" (Acts 9:2).[19] What was it about Antioch that led them to being called Christians, and that "Christians" is the name that stuck?

The passage itself provides three good clues. Antioch showed that disciples were "Christ ones," or "little Christs," because they evidenced God's grace (v. 23), because they were welcoming (v. 24), and because after a year of inspection they were seen to be genuine (v. 26).

In these three ways, Jesus disciples were clearly like him. And still today, grace, a welcoming spirit, and genuineness are magnetic hallmarks to a world that still longs for love, inclusion, and authenticity.

Prayer: God, work in me so that I may be a "Christ one" in the midst of those with whom I live and work. Amen.

━━

Week Nineteen, Day 1

Read John 14:6

Jesus described himself as the Way in conjunction with two other words: truth and life. Our look at Jesus as the Way will never be in isolation from these two, for when we see him as the Way, we will be simultaneously be encountering a truth that is life giving.

We will begin our exploration of Jesus as the Way at the widest place, in his opening statement, "I am." It was his way of affirming himself as one with God, a oneness he referred to more than once during his lifetime (e.g., John 10:30; 17:11). By using "I am" he was linking himself to Yahweh, something he did elsewhere too (John 8:58). His claim to equality with God led to his being crucified (John 5:18; Mark 14:61-64).

The additional words—way, truth, and life—must be viewed in relation to Jesus's identification of himself as the incarnation of God, the Word made flesh (John 1:14). This is both the scandal of Christ and the supremacy of Christ. Jesus is Lord. Jesus as the Way is one lens through which we look to see that.

Prayer: God, I say of Jesus what the Apostle Thomas said, "My Lord and my God" (John 20:28). Amen.

Week Nineteen, Day 2

Read John 14:6

When we hear the word *way*, we think immediately of a pathway, a roadway. A way is a means to get where we need to go. More than anything else, we need to go to God. Jesus is the Way to God.

Some theologically insert the word *only* into the text, making him say, "I am the only way." But the word is not in the text. We must discover what it means in terms of what he said himself, not what we say about him.[20]

Leaving things as Jesus said them, the Way is spacious, not constricted, and that is all the more clear when Way is an expression of who God is. God is the maker of "the heavens and the earth" (Genesis 1:1)—of everyone and everything (John 1:3). As the Way, Jesus is the incarnation of the universal, deep-and-wide, all-encompassing God. As the Way, Jesus invites us into largeness. Christ is all and in all (Colossians 3:11).

Prayer: God, following Jesus as the Way, I abandon my partialness and walk onto his "All-ness." Amen.

Week Nineteen, Day 3

Read John 14:6

By identifying himself as the Way, he was connecting himself with a reality that preceded him: the Tao. An extensive and rich experience awaits any who look at Jesus Christ through the wisdom of Taoism. We can only point to that in this meditation, saying what people like C. S. Lewis and Thomas Merton said, "Jesus is the Tao."

That "persons belonging to the Way" was the first name given to Jesus's disciples is further evidence that the person and work of Jesus was recognized as more than the words and deeds of a young rabbi in Israel. As the disciples fanned out across the world, people said, "We've heard this before . . . in a philosophy: the Tao. We did not know the Tao became a human being."

No wonder they wanted to learn more! Who wouldn't? When the universal Idea became flesh, the world received that as good news, and it was the mission, privilege, and joy of the disciples to say wherever they went, "Jesus is the gospel!" He still is.

Prayer: God, you gave me good news in a person, not a philosophy—in incarnation, not information. Amen.

Week Nineteen, Day 4

Read John 14:6

In what respects was Jesus the Way? We cannot be exhaustive in responding to the question because the Way is infinite; we can never say everything about him. The Way is also eternal; dimensions are still unfolding.

We can focus only on some key aspects.[21] We begin with Jesus as the Way of Love. Love is the essence of life, for the God of Life is love (1 John 4:8). Jesus loved fully from start to finish, and the words "his own" in John 13:1 are shown to be the wide swath of humanity. His love was so extensive it transformed the phrase "the chosen people" to mean everyone.

We cannot grasp this, we can only be grasped by it, so that we are liberated from our limited loving and transformed into those who love their neighbors as themselves (Matthew 22:39), who love the world as themselves (*Tao Te Ching*, 13).

Prayer: God, I see Jesus as the Way of Love. Amen.

Week Nineteen, Day 5

Read John 14:6

Jesus was the Way of simplicity. He called it being pure in heart (Matthew 5:8). This inner singularity produced the outer simplification Jesus described when he said that our lives are not defined by how much we have (Luke 12:15). Similarly, the Tao commends simplicity, "Reveal your simple self, embrace your original nature" (*Tao Te Ching*, 19).

The illustration for this simplicity was a child. Jesus said we would be kingdom-of-God people if we became like children (Matthew 18:3). Here too, he was voicing the Tao that said, "Being the stream of the universe, ever true and unswerving, become as a little child once more" (*Tao Te Ching*, 28).

Jesus's incarnation of simplicity is one we sorely need in a world where quantified materialism ("more is better") has become a defining value for many and even an article of faith for some Christians. But Jesus says that life is not evaluated by amount, and that the gospel is not linked to prosperity. Instead, the life of simplicity is the Way.

Prayer: God, take me past all my stuff to your way: the way of simplicity. Amen.

Week Twenty, Day 1

Read John 14:6

Jesus is the Way of reality, what some call the Perennial Tradition or the Great Way.[22] Jesus called it the kingdom of heaven, and in doing so he connected with the Tao (ultimate Reality).

Jesus said, "The kingdom of heaven is at hand" (Matthew 4:17 KJV), meaning available to everyone. Lao Tzu spoke similarly, that the Tao is "the common ancestor of all, the father of all things" (*Tao Te Ching*, chapter 4).

One of our great needs today is to regather this sense of universality, union, nonduality, and oneness. We have shattered reality into competitive fragments with jagged edges that wound. Jesus invites us to wholeness. Indeed, the word *salvation* means wholeness.

Prayer: God, I leave my "little kingdom" and head for the kingdom of heaven. Amen.

Week Twenty, Day 2

Read John 14:6

Jesus is the Way of wisdom. Paul described the excarnate Christ as the wisdom of God (1 Corinthians 1:24), and Jesus, the incarnate Christ, is identified as a wisdom teacher.[23] The Tao is all about wisdom, with numerous references to it in the *Tao Te Ching*.

In the sense of Way as path, Jesus is the road into wisdom. Wisdom is knowledge embraced and internalized. Wisdom is knowledge enacted and invested in day-to-day living. Wisdom is sacred simplicity that sees God everywhere and in everything.

In Christianity we call it experience, practical divinity (John Wesley), lived theology (Eugene Peterson), the Word made flesh in Jesus (John 1:14), and meant to be enfleshed in us as well (James 1:22). The Bible tells us to gain wisdom (Proverbs 4:7; 16:16). We seek for it and find it in Christ.

Prayer: God, you have shown me wisdom in Christ. Life "In Christ" will be my theme song. Amen.

Week Twenty, Day 3

Read John 14:6

Jesus is the Way of nonviolence. He is incarnated shalom, the word for pervasive peacefulness, comprehensive wellness. He also made it clear that this kind of peace is not automatic; it must be forged through effort. We must be peacemakers (Matthew 5:9).

Similarly, the Tao teaches that those who live by the Way "will oppose all conquest by force of arms" (*Tao Te Ching*, 30). The way this teaching is written makes it clear that even the *defeat* of evil must be through nonviolence—overcoming evil with good (Romans 12:21) through "the practice of the better" (Richard Rohr).[24]

Jesus modeled the nonviolent life,[25] to the point of refusing to insult those who insulted him (1 Peter 2:23), and telling us to put away our swords, or we would perish by them (Matthew 26:52). Indeed, the Way of Christ includes the pursuit of peace (1 Peter 3:11). It is an expression of the fruit of the Spirit (Galatians 5:22).

Prayer: God, I resolve to be a peacemaker. Amen.

Week Twenty, Day 4

Read John 14:6

Jesus is the Way of genuineness. He opposed hypocrisy, any form of life that created a false self or a counterfeit life. Pretending we are something we are not angered Jesus more than anything else. It creates the false self that not only poisons our soul, it also prevents us from seeing our need to be anything else.

Jesus said, "The kingdom of heaven is at hand" (Matthew 4:17 KJV), meaning available to everyone. Lao Tzu spoke similarly, that the Tao is "the common ancestor of all, the father of all things."[26]

Hypocrisy is something for everyone to avoid. It is a way of death, not life.

Prayer: God, I choose to be real with plenty to work on rather than choosing to be false and presuming I am A-OK with nothing to improve. Amen.

Week Twenty, Day 5

Read John 14:6

Jesus is the Way of revelation. Turning to the context in which John 14:6 is written, Jesus made it clear that he was the visible manifestation of the invisible God. He said that in seeing him we see the Father (John 14:9).

Similarly, the Tao Te Ching taught that "from the days of old till now its named, manifested forms have never ceased, by which we may view the father of all things" (*Tao Te Ching*, 21). Jesus, the wisdom teacher, was confirming that the supernatural is manifested in the natural. He did that in his parables (e.g., "the kingdom of heaven is like a mustard seed"), and he climaxed it by attributing it to his person.

In this connection, we reach the apex of revelation. We reach the revelation that John put into words, "the Word became flesh" (John 1:14).

Prayer: God, I see you in Jesus. I like what I see, and I want to honor what I see by becoming Christlike. Amen.

Week Twenty-one, Day 1

Read John 14:6

We have looked at selected ways that Jesus is the Way, the Tao incarnate. There are more, and the two parallel-saying books previously referenced will add to the picture. Today we move to the end of the verse where Jesus says, "No one comes to the Father except through me." We will spend this week looking at these words.

This is the most misunderstood verse in the Bible. It has been used to claim that the Christian faith is the only religion through which we can be saved, and that "believing in Jesus" is the only way to go to heaven. But, the fact is, this statement is not about either of those things. The context in which Jesus's words are found reveals what he meant, but we miss the meaning if we isolate the phrase from John 14:4-11.

We will complete this series on Jesus as the Way by looking at what he meant when he said, "no one comes to the Father except through me." If we are to understand Jesus as the Way, we must understand what he meant by these words.

Prayer: God, I open myself to Jesus as the Way—the Way to the Father. Amen.

Week Twenty-one, Day 2

Read John 14:4-11

Looking at the larger passage, the first thing we see is that it is not about who goes to heaven and who does not. Jesus's words in 14:6 are his response to a question asked by Thomas (v. 5) and a request by Philip (v. 8). The question was about where Jesus was going, and the request was for Jesus to show them the Father.

In other words, Jesus's words were not a general reference to who is saved and who is not. They were his way of telling the apostles important things about himself (14:6a) and his mission (14:6b). There is nothing in what he said about the superiority or exclusivity of Christianity.

Jesus spoke from two vantage points: as a Wisdom teacher and as the incarnate Christ. We have looked at his Wisdom side in 14:6a; we now look at his Christ side in 14:6b. And the context shows his mission was to reveal the Father and take us to him. This is where we begin in understanding the meaning of "no one comes to the Father except through me."

Prayer: God, thank you for giving us the Christ in human form, so we can know you and be with you. Amen.

Week Twenty-one, Day 3

Read John 14:4-11

As the incarnate Christ, Jesus was pointing to the excarnate Christ, the universal Christ—for Christians, the second person of the Trinity. As such, he is the way, truth, and life for all. Christ is all (ultimate) and in all (universal) as Colossians 3:11 says. He said this about himself (John 12:32), and Paul wrote similarly (1 Corinthians 15:22; Ephesians 1:9-10; and Colossians 1:20).

The metaphor for this universality is in Jesus's own words, "I am the light of the world" (John 8:12). E. Stanley Jones wrote about this, "The light that was in conscience, in insight, in illumination, in ideals, was the light of the excarnate Christ. If people lived according to that 'light,' they will be saved and saved by Christ, however unconscious they may have been of Him as Christ."[27] This means his words "no one comes to the Father except through me" are not about who goes to heaven and who does not. They are not an exclusion.

Prayer: God, I see that my salvation is one part of your plan of salvation for all. Amen.

Week Twenty-one, Day 4

Read John 14:4-11

Having freed Jesus's words in 14:6 from exclusivity and restored them to their intended universality, we can now turn specifically to the words "comes to" in 14:6b.

The Greek word is not a word about arriving in a place (e.g., "comes to heaven"), but rather about recognizing something. In this sense, Jesus was saying, "People come to recognize God as Father through me." E. Stanley Jones saw this and wrote, "Jesus puts a face on God."[28]

The Old Testament had a view of God as Father (e.g., Malachi 2:10), but it was a concept. In Jesus, the principle became a person; the idea became an individual. That's what Jesus told Philip in 14:9-11.

We are living in a time when abstract theology about God has lost much of its appeal. We need an "enfleshed" theology that shows us who God is. We have it in Jesus, the Word made flesh (John 1:14).

Prayer: God, I see you because I have seen Jesus. Amen.

Week Twenty-one, Day 5

Read John 14:6

We have spent three weeks exploring one sentence that Jesus spoke. We've done so because, as William Temple said, if our concept of God is wrong, things go from bad to worse.

Letting the context of John 14:4-11 be the interpreter for John 14:6, we see Jesus was the incarnate Christ speaking from the vantage point of the excarnate Christ. Jesus did this as a wisdom teacher; indeed, as the Tao incarnate. He told us that Christ is the way, truth, and life—for all.

He told us that when we see him, we come to recognize God is our heavenly Father.

This is not masculinizing God; it is personalizing God. God is transgender, and the Bible gives to God both masculine and feminine qualities—all in the effort to say that our relationship with God is I-Thou, not I-It. We are loved personally by God who is Person. We are God's beloved children, and we can love a God who looks like Jesus. This God is the way, the truth, and the life for us all!

Prayer: God, you are the way, truth, and life for me in Christ, and in him I come to see you as you are. Amen.

❧❧

Week Twenty-two, Day 1

Read Psalm 8:4-5

"Slightly less" ("a little lower," KJV) is a good intermediate point for understanding who we are. Left to ourselves we tend to think too highly of ourselves . . . or not highly enough. We end up drowning in pride or despair. The Bible steers a middle path, and it is the path of life.

"Slightly less" holds our sacredness and our submission in a healthy relationship. We kneel before the Lord our Maker, but we do so as God's beloved children. Our "glory and grandeur" is real, just not ultimate. We can hold our heads high, while keeping our eyes on highest heaven.

This is humanity as God created it to be, and makes us people as God wills for us to be. This is holiness that combines spirit, soul, and body (1 Thessalonians 5:23) in a way that gives to our humanity its sacred worth without leading us to think we can be our own god.

Prayer: God, I come before you as your beloved child, and I do so on my knees. Amen.

Week Twenty-two, Day 2

Read 1 Thessalonians 5:23

Our sacred humanity exists in a "three-in-one" nature akin to the trinitarian nature of God. We are spirit, soul, and body. Now is a good time to look at each aspect.

We are spirit. It is here where we are most like God. Jesus said, "God is a spirit" (John 4:24). Invisibility and eternality are two key attributes of spirit. In the same way, who we are is essentially invisible—that is, not defined by what we eat or wear, or by how much we have. Jesus said that too (Matthew 5:25; Luke 12:15). Paul said the same when he wrote that our lives are hidden with Christ in God (Colossians 3:3).

As spirit, we are also eternal. Again, like Jesus, we have come from God and we will return to God (John 13:3). Whatever eternity is, we will live in it. Forever. Taken together invisibility and eternality reveal our inestimable worth—a value that cannot be measured by any earthly standard, and one that never comes to an end.

Prayer: God, because I am spirit I will never again use a secondary means to asses my worth or my longevity. Amen.

Week Twenty-two, Day 3

Read 1 Thessalonians 5:23

We are soul. Of the three dimensions of our humanity, this one is the most difficult because the soul exists with a foot in spirit and another in body—a mediator between the two. The soul is not pure spirit, but it intuits things of the spirit. The soul is not material, but it sends and receives signals from the material.

One way to put it is that the soul is intuitive toward the spiritual and sensate toward the physical. And as such, it is the meeting place of heaven and earth in our being. Simply put, because we are soul, we can relate to God and think about heaven. Because we are soul, we can apply eternal truths to our temporal lives.

One word often used for the soul is *mind*, though this means more than rational cognition. It is more like the word *mindful*—that is, because we are soul, we can be filled with the knowledge of God (Colossians 1:9), and being thus filled, we can be fully aware of and active in the things of God.

Prayer: God, because I am soul, I have a capacity to relate to you, and a will to do your will on earth as it is in heaven. Amen.

Week Twenty-two, Day 4

Read 1 Thessalonians 5:23

We are body. An amazing network of cells, nerves, tissues, and fibers—organs and systems. All God-made and God-sustained.

Our bodies will not last forever; they don't have to because our spirit dimension has that covered. Nevertheless, we are called to care for our bodies because they are inhabited by the Spirit (1 Corinthians 6:19) and they produce the Spirit's fruit (Galatians 5:22-23).

73

Our bodies are the reminder that spirituality includes physicality. Our love and our lives matter. Our piety and our politics are important. Praying and playing are holy. Our blood pressure and our devotion to God need to be in good shape. Self-care honors the God who made us.

The spiritual life is a whole-life enterprise. There is no part that stands alone. God is in everything, and in every part of us. Our entire life is meant to be a hallelujah.

Prayer: God, I am yours—top to bottom, inside and out. Amen.

Week Twenty-two, Day 5

Read 1 Thessalonians 5:23

Our tripartite nature is as singular and natural as God's trinitarian nature is. Our human life is a perichoresis (circle dance) like God's divine life. Our spirit, soul, and body are in concert.

Unfortunately, we see people who exaggerate one aspect of their lives to the neglect of others. Some people are (as is said) so heavenly minded that they are of no earthly good. And others are so earthy there's no hint of heaven to be found. Caricatures of any kind create a false humanity.

As we complete this brief look at our humanity, it is good to remember that the meaning of the word *salvation* is wholeness. We are reverently and marvelously made so that every aspect of our lives can glorify and serve God. And that twofold potential is where we find our purpose and our joy.

Prayer: God, I sing, "take my life—my entire life—and let it be, consecrated Lord, to thee." Amen.

Week Twenty-three, Day 1

Read Galatians 6:4

Physical death occurs in many ways. Spiritual death does too. One form of spiritual death is comparing ourselves with others. Comparison leads us to pride or to despair, thinking we are doing more than others, or less.

Paul says we are to avoid comparing ourselves with others and instead "be happy with doing a good job" in whatever work we are doing. Our joy comes in being faithful to our task. That's all that matters.

The Covenant Service used particularly by Christians in the Wesleyan tradition has this simple reminder, "Christ has many services to be done."[29] Each of us provides one of those services. The validation of our service is not how it stacks up compared with what others are doing, but that it is done "for the good of all" (6:10). If what we do accomplishes that, it is godly work.

Prayer: God, I accept my task as your assignment. All I want is to do it well. Amen.

Week Twenty-three, Day 2

Read Matthew 16:13-19

When we read this passage, we usually focus on Peter's answer, and that's a good thing to do. But today, we will concentrate on Jesus's question, noticing that he asked it about two different groups—the general public and the disciples.

Notice the answers are different. The general public gave a secondhand response; the disciples gave one (via Peter) based on daily contact. The way we see people differs depending on whether we observe them from afar or whether we view them up close and personal. The correct answer came from firsthand interaction.

We would do well to decide who others are on the basis of a personal relationship with them. Native Americans call it walking a mile in another's moccasins. We almost always see people differently once we get to know them. Our most correct assessments emerge from our associations. The next time we hear someone talk about someone else, or find ourselves doing so, we should stop and ask, "Is this coming from hearsay or friendship?"

Prayer: Dear God, I will not claim to know who someone is until I take the time to get to know them. Amen.

Week Twenty-three, Day 3

Read Ecclesiastes 3:1-8

We have some things in common. Time is one of them. We have the same amount of time as everyone else. We have a common purpose as well—to make the best use of the time we have been given.

Each moment comes to us as a gift, and also as a task. The opportunities and responsibilities vary, but the challenge is the same—to use each moment in a way that enriches us and others.

The writer of Ecclesiastes described it as discerning how to enjoy the moment and to use it for good (3:22). Jesus said that time is an invitation to see and to hear what is going on and align ourselves with it (Mark 8:18). Both ways of living in time are ways of wisdom—not just observing time, but enriching it. In this very moment, we all have the time to do that.

Prayer: God, I accept this moment in time as both a gift and a task. Amen.

Week Twenty-three, Day 4

Read Mark 8:18

Jesus's great desire for his disciples was that we can not only see things, but more, see into things, through them, and beyond them. Jesus did this over and over with people, places, and things.

When he later talked about the end of the age, people fell into two groups: those who could see, and those who could not (Matthew 25:31-46). The kind of sight he desired is the ability to be moved to care.

Compassion is the sign that we see. The sight Jesus wants us to have is this: paying attention to life until we no longer see it as something separated from us, but rather looking at life until we see ourselves in what's going on. When we see ourselves inside the circle of life, we will then see that we are to live for Christ wherever and however we can. We have "eyes to see" when we ask Christ, "What can I do for you in this situation?"

Prayer: God, give me eyes to see so that I see every moment and an opportunity to live for you. Amen.

Week Twenty-three, Day 5

Read Ephesians 4:22-24

Like Jesus, Paul used everyday things to teach eternal truths. He wrote to the Ephesians, comparing becoming Christian to changing clothes. The idea carries numerous insights.

Becoming a disciple of Christ is an ordinary experience, not defined or marked by spectacular occurrences. Becoming a follower of Christ is a willful exchange of bad things for good ones; it's a choice anyone can make. Moreover, living for Jesus is an ongoing process. We change clothes daily, and at certain times, we outgrow the clothing and have to wear a new size. Then too, we wear clothing for the season we're in.

Each of these ideas can be expanded and enriched. But Paul's simplicity is enough to say, "You can do this." And as we read the rest of his Letter to the Ephesians, he goes on to say, "If you do this, you'll be glad you did."

Prayer: God, thanks for giving me the desire to change clothes and for giving me new clothes to wear. Amen.

❧❧

Week Twenty-four, Day 1

Read Luke 18:9-14

We learn a lot about prayer from the Bible, including how not to pray. This passage shows us what bad prayer looks and sounds like. It looks like posturing, and it sounds like pride.

It's summed up in the Pharisee's words, "God, I thank you that I am not like everyone else." Bad prayer blinds us to the truth. The Pharisee was, in fact, like everyone else—and so are we (e.g., Romans 3:23). Bad prayer separates us from others, and leaves us feeling good to be so separated. Bad prayer is self-referent. In a nutshell, bad prayer is arrogant.

Instead of this, genuine prayer keeps us humble, connected, and graced. It is God-referent. All this is captured in the word *mercy*. In a nutshell, good prayer is restorative. And Jesus left no doubt about it, the tax collector, not the Pharisee, left the temple justified (restored and renewed).

Prayer: God, show mercy to me, a sinner. Amen.

Week Twenty-four, Day 2

Read Luke 12:19

The farmer in Jesus's parable obviously worked hard. It has never been easy to do everything necessary to produce a bumper crop, harvest it, and store it away. Jesus did not say anything negative about that. Hard work is commendable.

The problem was, the farmer became self-sufficient in the midst of his work. And more, he became greedy. That's what Jesus condemned, a foolish attitude because it described a person who saw his success as a "what's in it for me?" attitude.

History is replete with examples of those who treat their prosperity as for them only. The downward spiral moves from success, to greed, to elitism—where our abundance is not shared. When we view our life as something we possess rather than as something we share, we become foolish just like the farmer was.

Prayer: God, give me a generous heart. Amen.

Week Twenty-four, Day 3

Read Acts 17:22

Spiritual maturity includes the ability and the willingness to receive truth from anyone. Thomas Aquinas wrote, "Every truth without exception—and whoever may utter it—is from the Holy Spirit." Paul recognized this as he walked around Athens, and he acknowledged what he found in his opening remark to the council on Mars Hill.

Unfortunately, there are some people who only accept truth from their "approved sources." They steer people away from those who think differently from the way they do. Truth limiters give the impression that they have everything anyone could ever need, portraying themselves as the "one-stop shopping center" for truth.

Some go so far as to ban books (and other things), shaming or punishing any who seek truth elsewhere.

But truth is truth, and the whole world is full of it. The search for truth and the discovery of it is a deep-and-wide process. We probe our own tradition deeply, and we explore other traditions widely. As we do so, our storehouse of truth is expanded and enriched.

Prayer: God, I seek your truth everywhere. Amen.

Week Twenty-four, Day 4

Read Acts 17:28

God accepts us where we are. We see this in the way Paul shared the gospel with the Athenians. Beginning by honoring them (v. 22), he built on what they already knew and accepted to be true (vv. 23-27). He brought it all together in today's verse.

From it we understand that we exist in God. Our life is within God's Life. We do not have to be people of faith for this to be so. It is so by virtue of our creation, complete with a miraculous variety of systems in our bodies that sustain us and enable us to do amazing things.

The Bible never separates flesh and spirit; it only asks us to use our lives as windows through which to look to see ourselves "living, moving, and existing" in God. We inhabit by means of the natural, but we are only explained by the supernatural.

Prayer: God, I am because you are. Amen.

Week Twenty-four, Day 5

Read Isaiah 29:13

Fickle. It's not a word we use a lot today. But it is the one-word description of the condition Isaiah was writing about. It's the disconnect between our beliefs and our behaviors. It is arguably the main problem we have to deal with. It's one that Ezekiel (33:31), Jesus (Matthew 15:18), James (2:17), the first Christians (Acts 5:1-10), and later Christians (e.g., Clement of Rome) identified as the essence of hypocrisy.

There will always be a gap between our profession of faith and our expression of it. We never get it right all the time. But the problem occurs when we act as if the gap isn't there—or worse, try to make others believe we are living the faith when, in fact, we are not doing so.

The fact is, the general public sees the hypocrisy better than we do. Fickleness casts a spell on our spirit. We only awaken from it when we are either willing to confess our duplicity or have it called out by someone, or both. However it happens, congruence must be our desire.

Prayer: God, give me grace so that my inward and outward life match up. Amen.

***

Week Twenty-five, Day 1

Read Matthew 4:12–5:13

There are passages in the Bible that encapsulate the gospel. The Beatitudes are one of them, along with the rest of the Sermon on the Mount. We begin an extended look at them today.

But in order to see them clearly, we must go back into Matthew 4. The Beatitudes are the result of a process Jesus was initiating, summed up in the words *repent, recruit,* and *reveal.* Repentance was Jesus's way of asking, "Are you willing to look at life in a new way?" Recruitment was his way of asking, "Do you believe I can lead you into that new life?" Revealing was his way of showing that life through his deeds and words. The Beatitudes are the port of entry into abundant living.

The Beatitudes are wisdom teaching, revealing that the life of God in the human soul comes to pass by a descent/ascent journey. The first three beatitudes describe the descent, the fourth beatitude is the turning point, and the final four beatitudes portray the ascent. We commence this transforming journey tomorrow.

Prayer: God, I am willing to look at life in a new way, to follow you, and to learn from you what life is. Amen.

Week Twenty-five, Day 2

Read Matthew 5:3

We don't use the phrase "poor in spirit" today, but it is where Jesus said the abundant life begins, so we need to understand what he was talking about.

Today, we speak of this emptying as humility. It is dethroning egotism (the false self) so that we can live for God alone. The classical word for this is *renunciation*. It means saying, "It's not all about me."

Jesus began the Beatitudes by saying, "Your problem is that you are full of yourself, so much so that God gets all but crowded out. You've been trying to be your own god, but there is only one God—and you're not it. Give it up!"

Poverty of spirit is the essential emptying that clears the shelves of our soul, replacing "the works of the flesh" (selfishness) with the fruit of the Spirit (godliness). Being poor in spirit is coming to God empty-handed so that God can fill them. Poverty of spirit is paradox: we find our life by losing it (Matthew 10:39). We live in the kingdom of heaven.

Prayer: God, I take myself out of my hands and put myself into your hands, where I belong. Amen.

Week Twenty-five, Day 3

Read Matthew 5:4

The mourning Jesus is referring to is more the kind we do when someone we love dies. Of course, God comforts us then, and we are grateful for God's presence when we grieve. But Jesus has something else in mind here.

The mourning in the second beatitude is what we call "godly sorrow." About what? That we lived for so long acting as if we were gods. The second beatitude flows from the first one. We mourn that we lived without being poor in spirit. Mourning is a sign that we regret having lived selfishly; it's the evidence that we now have a contrite heart (Psalm 51:17).

This kind of mourning increases our resolve to live for God alone—the mourning that makes our renunciation in the first beatitude more than a fleeting thing. This is mourning that produces grit, not guilt. We are comforted—that is, given strength (fortis) to develop our initial commitment into a way of life.

Prayer: God, I am truly sorry that I lived so long like I was a god—so sorry, in fact, that I never intend to live that way again. Give me strength to make good on this promise. Amen.

Week Twenty-five, Day 4

Read Matthew 5:5

We hear the word *meekness*, and we can easily think of it as weakness. It is the opposite; it is strength under control. The first two beatitudes place us in God's hands with the resolve to remain there. In the third beatitude we offer all that we are and have to God, to be used as God sees fit.

Meekness is the consecration of our life to God. We become what Paul called "living sacrifices" (Romans 12:1). We capture the meaning of the third beatitude when we sing the hymn, "Take My Life, and Let It Be Consecrated."

The fourth beatitude develops our commitment into a life-style, as the hymn says, all our moments and days—our silver and our gold—and ultimately our will, so that in everything our greatest desire and joy is to be instruments of God's peace.

Prayer: God, you've got me! Now, use me as you like; it's what I want more than anything else. Amen.

Week Twenty-five, Day 5

Read Matthew 5:6

This beatitude is the pivot from descent to ascent. It acknowledges appetite (hunger and thirst) and envisions the satisfaction of it (righteousness). This beatitude marks the turning point in our spiritual journey.

Emptying is necessary, but it must be followed with filling. Emptying creates the space for God to bless us with new life. It is good to recognize our hunger and thirst, but unless we eat and drink, we will starve to death.

Unfortunately, there is a spirituality that focuses on prohibitions. But without subsequent permissions, we become negative, legalistic, judgmental, and bitter. Healthy spirituality moves us from a no to a yes—a divine yes. The Beatitudes model the transition.

It is a journey into righteousness—an idea that describes inward and outward life. The final four beatitudes illustrate what righteousness looks like.

Prayer: God, I am ready to satisfy my hunger and thirst for life with the things that make it satisfying. Amen.

◆◆

Week Twenty-six, Day 1

Read Matthew 5:7

The first step on "the upward way" is being merciful. Compassion is the universal sign (taught in all religions) that we are no longer living for ourselves.

Mercy is an important way to describe this kind of living because it is compassion based on grace. Mercy does not give people what they deserve; it gives them what they need. Mercy means discovering, not assuming—listening before speaking—asking before deciding. In the Native American tradition, mercy is walking a mile in another's moccasins.

Compassion is acting in response to what's going on in other people's lives, especially what's missing in their lives. Compassion forgives, heals, restores, and provides. Being merciful is a long-haul mindset, not a quick-fix program. Compassion is the sign that we are living our lives for the sake of others.

Prayer: God, yours is a heart of compassion. Give me that heart too. Amen.

Week Twenty-six, Day 2

Read Matthew 5:8

Purity of heart is not utter cleanliness, it's singularity. A "clean heart" is one that seeks the will of God above everything else.

Christian perfection is not flawlessness, it's wanting the ways of the kingdom of God to be realized on the earth.

Jesus said that when this is our heart's desire, we will "see God." This is not a literal vision, it is a discernment of how God is present and active among us.

And there's more: when we see God, we follow God. This beatitude is an indication of our desire to be instruments of God's peace. This beatitude is about becoming cocreators with God. It is a seeing that becomes a serving.

The wonderful thing is that when we see God, we see God in every moment, in everyone, and in every place. When we do that, we recognize that we do not want to wait or go someplace else to live the spiritual life. The opportunities for doing so are here and now.

Prayer: God, I see you—all the time and all over the place. What a vision! Amen.

Week Twenty-six, Day 3

Read Matthew 5:9

Peace-making is one of the great needs of our time. But that has been the case most of the time. The absence of peace runs through human history. God's search for peacemakers is perennial.

Offering ourselves to be peacemakers is a hallmark of the blessed life according to Jesus. Saint Francis captured it, beginning his now-classic prayer asking, "Lord, make me an instrument of your peace," and then going on to list specific ways for being such a person.

The enlightening word is *instrument*. We are individual tools God uses to restore peace where it is absent. We fit different contexts and serve particular purposes, promoting peace through little acts that have the potential to connect with others who are doing the same, and thus advancing the cause of peace on the earth.

In doing so, Jesus says, we are children of God—people in whom love prevails and overcomes evil with good, restoring shalom wherever and however we can.

Prayer: God, you are peace. As your child, I will be a peacemaker. Amen.

Week Twenty-six, Day 4

Read Matthew 5:10-11

The gospel is countercultural. If we proclaim it, we will receive pushback. Imperialism (egotism/ethnocentrism) retaliates when it is resisted.

The final beatitude is the only one Jesus amplified. He did this to make it clear that following him is no easy thing. To live for him means that we speak and act in ways that go against the grain. The blessed life is intrinsically prophetic, and prophets are always persecuted in some way—sometimes by fellow believers who have watered down their faith and compromised their convictions.

But here's the thing: we are persecuted "for righteousness' sake." Sadly, some people think they are being prophetic when they are only being obnoxious. Prophets stay within the context of blessedness—inside the circle where love prevails. The gospel life takes courage, but it is not caustic. Nevertheless, when we advocate the values of God above those of the fallen world, we will not be well received. The final beatitude describes the reality that accompanies faithfulness.

Prayer: God, I understand what I am getting into. It is good, but not easy. I get it. Amen.

Week Twenty-six, Day 5

Read Matthew 5:3-11

The eight beatitudes are woven together into a singular life by the word *blessed*. It is a rich word in its Hebrew, Greek, and Aramaic versions. The blessed life is the life we are made for and yearn for. It is the life that brings joy and fulfillment.

But to be blessed is also to be accountable and responsible. The blessed life is not stored up, it is given away. If we think of the beatitudes as seeds, we will recognize that each of them is meant to bear fruit. Each one is intended to enhance the common good.

We must not miss the fact that Jesus described the blessed life to a multitude, not to an individual. The blessed life is life together. Jesus was creating a community; his teaching can be personally received, but it must be collectively preserved.

Prayer: God, I receive the way of life you are offering me, and I resolve that it will not end with me. Amen.

Week Twenty-seven, Day 1

Read Matthew 5:3-11

The Beatitudes are not separate from the rest of the Sermon on the Mount. The rest of Jesus's message is an extension and an expansion of the life he described in the Beatitudes. Indeed, the entirety of his teachings is connected to them. A profitable exercise is to read the remainder of Jesus's sermon, connecting what he went on to say with one or more of the Beatitudes. It will become clear that they are the template for the message.

We need organizing principles, pegs on which to hang the details of our lives. The Beatitudes (and the rest of the Sermon on the Mount) ask and answer these questions, "What is the life God wills for us?" and "How does this life manifest itself in daily living?" In the end we come to see that the blessed life saturates every aspect of life and every moment of our existence.

Prayer: God, like a sponge I will soak in the blessed life you have for me, and then I will move through my days squeezing it out for the sake of others. Amen.

Week Twenty-seven, Day 2

Read Psalm 14:2-3

Unlike some national histories, the Bible does not sanitize its main characters. Moses was a murderer. Jacob was a cheater. Rahab was a harlot. David was an adulterer. Peter denied Jesus; the disciples abandoned him. Paul persecuted Christians. Euodia and Syntyche couldn't get along. And on and on.

None of this is in the Bible to excuse sin; it's there to prevent perfectionism or the creation of what Thomas Merton called "plaster saints."[30] In fact, the Bible goes out of its way to call out pretense.

The biblical story is about grace—about mercy given to us "while we were yet sinners" (Romans 5:8 KJV). The spiritual life is messy, and that is precisely what keeps it from being taken over by falsehood and hypocrisy. Realism preserves humility. In a word, spirituality is reality, and that gives rise to both confession and hope.

Prayer: God, thank you for accepting me just as I am while working to make me better. Amen.

Week Twenty-seven, Day 3

Read Hebrews 13:7

Our predecessors are not meant to be relics of the past, but rather revelations of how holiness is applied to current reality. Each of the saints worked out their salvation in the context of their day and time. The lessons we glean from them are meant not only to be remembered but also reenacted. As the writer of Hebrews put it, we are to imitate their faith.

The "great cloud of witnesses" (Hebrews 12:1) bear individual testimony to faith lived in particular times and places. Together they give a collective witness to the relevance and transferability of faith from one generation to another.

It is good for us to stop from time to time and ask what gifts we have been given by those who have influenced us most. And once we recall them, the next step is to consider how we might use those gifts in our present and specific circumstances. Virtues rot on the tree if left there. Godliness is not an antique, it is a manifestation for the common good here and now.

Prayer: God, I will honor those who have influenced me by living like them in my time. Amen.

Week Twenty-seven, Day 4

Read Psalm 46:1-3

We need help. Life often comes at us with challenges too big to handle. Even as a king, with wealth and power at his fingertips, David recognized this, and did not hesitate to ask God for help.

Sometimes God gives us additional strength to "power through" our dilemma. But sometimes God offers us a refuge.

Wise people do not consider it a weakness to recognize their limitations and to seek shelter from storms they cannot overcome.

Hunkering down is an act of faith, a sign that we understand "times of trouble" to be temporary. Hiding out in God is an indication that we know where our ultimate security lies. Asking for help is a primary form of prayer, and the sooner we do it, the better off we'll be.

Prayer: God, truth be told, I need you every hour. Help me in each moment, sometimes with strength and sometimes with refuge. Amen.

Week Twenty-seven, Day 5

Isaiah 41:10-14

Courage does not come out of nowhere. It comes from the confidence that God is with us. It is increased by experience, as we discover that God has given us strength when we needed it.

Courage is one of the gifts of aging. We increasingly experience God's presence and provision. Courage becomes an expression of trust—that God's grace, given to us in the past, will be given to us again in the present.

On the other hand, courage is always a test of our resolve. Challenges come with no guarantees of success. In this sense, courage is believing that doing the right thing will be attended by God's mercy.

Most of all, courage is the conviction that nothing can separate us from God's love. We do what is called for even when we must do so against the tide of opposition and even suffering. Courage is the will to say "No matter what, I will seek to do God's will."

Prayer: God, I have courage because I have you. And that is enough. Amen.

❧❧

Week Twenty-eight, Day 1

Read 1 Corinthians 15:58

We live in a world of speed. Technology evolves partly based on its ability to accomplish tasks faster and faster. Our minds follow suit, generating increasing expectations for rapid solutions and quick fixes.

But the problems of life are not solved by speed; they are overcome by steadfastness. God's call is for us to be people who stand firm and endure. We must be unshaken when things are not resolved quickly. Lasting achievements unfold over time; progress occurs little by little.

Inventors and explorers know this. Artists know this. We must cultivate the mindset of tenacity. We must stick to the tasks we feel called to accomplish rather than flitting from one thing to another. And even then, we will often have to hand off our work to a new generation who can pick up where we left off and carry on. Steadfastness can be fulfilling once we realize that there's more to life than speed.

Prayer: God, I mark my life with faithfulness, not by being fast. Amen.

Week Twenty-eight, Day 2

Read Luke 10:38-42

We continue to speculate about what Jesus meant when he said, "One thing is necessary." We know he loved Mary and Martha (John 11:5), so he did not say it to favor Mary over Martha. The statement meant something else.

It likely meant that living in the present moment is the one necessary thing. Martha was distracted by her perceived need to get dinner ready (v. 41), and her shift of focus took her away from Jesus. She traded in attentiveness for anticipation. Had she stayed put like Mary did, Jesus might have said, "Let's go out for dinner tonight. I'm buying." But her thinking that she had to fix dinner moved her out of the present moment into an assumed future. Martha did nothing wrong, but she missed the moment in a way Mary did not.

When we live outside the present moment, we may not do anything wrong, but we live by assumptions more than actualities. From there it is easy to be like Martha, becoming "worried and distracted by many things." Staying attentive to Jesus in the present moment is the one necessary thing.

Prayer: God, I will stay with you, here and now. Amen.

Week Twenty-eight, Day 3

Read Romans 12

There are times when it feels as if there is nothing we can say or do that makes any difference in the grand scheme of things. Nothing changes; the world moves on as if we were not even here. When we feel this way, this chapter in Paul's Letter to the Romans is our go-to passage.

Paul says there is a lot we can do . . . should do . . . must do. It begins in the offering of ourselves to God as people through whom God can work (vv. 1-2). It continues in using our gifts for good (vv. 3-8). And then, it proliferates into multiple specific attitudes and actions, summed up in the phrase, "defeat evil with good" (vv. 9-21).

After we read this passage, we can never again think that our lives are insignificant, any more than a raindrop can believe its wetness doesn't matter. We are always in a larger body; more is going on than what we can see or even imagine. We have one calling: to be faithful in our time and place. These verses help us understand what that means and how to do it.

Prayer: God, what I can do, I will do. And I will do it all for you. Amen.

Week Twenty-eight, Day 4

Read Colossians 3:17

We live from our motives. We enact our convictions. Our tongues, hands, and feet follow our hearts (Matthew 15:19). Paul's words take this principle and apply it to all of life in the word *whatever*.

We keep trying to compartmentalize faith to certain days and to "religious" topics. But the Bible will not let us do that. The message is this: faith is pervasive. We are called to live for Christ in every area of life.

God does not want a tip of our hat, but rather an inclination of our heart. We are not meant to be ceremonial, but committed. And the evidence of our commitment is found in the little things—in the "whatever" of our life.

Prayer: God, I will live for you in "whatever" ways I can. Amen.

Week Twenty-eight, Day 5

Read John 19:30

Theologians have developed multiple theories of the atonement in the attempt to explain what it means. They all boil down to one message: atonement is the one-word revelation that God will not allow anyone or anything to have the final word over us.

God alone has that word, and Jesus spoke it, "It is finished!" (v. 30 NRSVue). God's aim—the redemption of everyone and everything (1 Corinthians 15:22)—has been achieved. In Christ, "all" have been made alive. There is no way we can take ourselves out of that picture. God, the Divine Artist, has painted us into it.

Nothing can separate us from the love of God in Christ Jesus (Romans 8:31-39). We have been reconciled to God through Christ (Colossians 1:20). The atonement has established the trajectory of salvation when God will "gather up" all things in Christ (Ephesians 1:10 NRSVue). We will never receive any news better than this!

Prayer: God, in Christ's atonement I hear you saying, "I love you." I will live in a way that says, "I love you too." Amen.

Week Twenty-nine, Day 1

Read 1 Corinthians 3:6

Sidewalks are built in sections. No section encompasses the whole path, but each one contributes to it. The purpose of each section is to facilitate the journey in its specific place.

Our lives are like that. We are sections in God's sidewalk, a path none of us sees entirely. We cannot see where it began or where it will end. We can only see our time and place, but we share a common purpose with every other section—to be strong so that travelers can continue their journey.

The Bible calls this faithfulness. It is a mark of discipleship (Luke 16:10) and part of the fruit of the Spirit (Galatians 5:22). It means tending our time and place in the name of Christ. We understand that we are sections in God's path, and we find our joy in playing our part in God's ongoing plan.

Prayer: God, I ask for nothing more than to be faithful to you in my time and place. Amen.

Week Twenty-nine, Day 2

Read 1 Timothy 4:7

Everything in our life that goes the way we want it to go is the result of sustained effort, which usually begins clumsily but with improvement as time goes by. We become good at those things we practice.

The spiritual life is no exception. By virtue of being made in the image of God, we are all spiritual. The question is whether or not we are living formatively or deformatively. It depends on the extent to which we practice the means of grace (the spiritual disciplines) that make the spiritual life real, not just imagined.

Paul calls this "training," to be godly, not just hoping to be. The image is the gym, where we "work out" our faith, strengthening it and invigorating it. Living the Christian life happens just like everything else beneficial does—by training, not just trying.

Prayer: God, I will practice my faith, not just profess it. Amen.

Week Twenty-nine, Day 3

Philippians 2:12

When we are relating to the Eternal God, it doesn't matter whether we have been Christians for thirty minutes or thirty years. We can always take another step in faith. We never come to the end of knowing and growing in our relationship with an infinite God.

Paul's word is the reminder that every facet of our faith is partial. Every aspect of the spiritual life is a step in the journey. Our task is to receive God's grace and cultivate it.

We do this, Paul says, with reverence and care. That is, we recognize the sacredness of our relationship with God, and we develop it as good stewards of the precious gift that it is. We do this, not with a somber sense of duty, but with the celebratory note of opportunity. Every experience we have with God is precious in itself, and also a doorway into something more.

Prayer: God I am grateful for everything you have done for me. I will show it by using it as a means to experience even more of you. Amen.

Week Twenty-nine, Day 4

Read Matthew 24:13

As technology enables us to do things faster and faster, we increasingly develop a quick-fix mindset. Problems must be solved quickly. We can come to view the Christian experience the same way. We develop six-week studies and deliverable formulas for the spiritual life.

Jesus tells us to look at our spiritual formation differently. We are running a marathon not a sprint. The spiritual life is more nearly a sunrise than a lightning bolt. We are in this for the long haul. Endurance is the word for it.

This perspective helps us in two ways. First, it saves us from perfectionism, thinking we have to "get it done" right the first time around. And second, it prevents pessimism, thinking "it isn't working." When we place our experience with God in the context of endurance, we can relax, setting our advances and setbacks in the context of the up-and-down, success-and-failure realities of spiritual growth. Endurance saves us from becoming prideful when we get it right and despairing when we get it wrong. Endurance keeps us going.

Prayer: God, I will keep going, one day at a time, with you. Amen.

Week Twenty-nine, Day 5

Read Romans 8:38

This is one of the verses in scripture that can be misread easily. Paul is not saying that nothing can come between us and God's love. All kinds of things can do that. Some things that do so are no fault of our own. At other times, we erect the barriers. The way between us and God is not always clear.

We can understand this verse by looking at nature. Clouds can hide the sun, but they do not extinguish it. There are times when we cannot see the sun or feel its warmth, but it is still there. In the same way, we do not always "feel the love" of God, but that does not mean it has ceased to exist.

This verse is a reminder that God does not give love and withhold it. God loves all the time, no matter what. This verse offers the foundation of hope that we need to stand on when our sense of being loved by God isn't there. Like the sun's light, God's love never ceases.

Prayer: God, I will continue to believe you love me whether I can feel it or not. Amen.

❦

Week Thirty, Day 1

Read Matthew 15:19

The world says, "You are what you do." And that's true. Our actions shape us, especially as we repeat them. Acts turn into patterns over time.

This verse speaks another truth, "You do what you are." Conduct is the product of character. Our hands move at the impulse of our heart. The heart is a well from which we draw the water we call our words and deeds. We drink from the wells we dig.

In another analogy in John 15, Jesus said the same. Fruit comes from a root. Our lives reveal where we're rooted. The spiritual life is "living from the heart." Spiritual formation begins in the establishment of virtue, what we often refer to as the fruit of the Spirit (Galatians 5:22-23). Each word simultaneously describes our inner mind and our outward manner.

Prayer: God, shape me inwardly so that I may live for you outwardly. Amen.

Week Thirty, Day 2

Read Romans 8:21

Redemption is not limited to God's saving of people, it is about God saving the whole creation, from the smallest particle to the farthest star—with everyone and everything in between.

This is nothing out of the ordinary. God's covenant is all inclusive (Genesis 9:9-17), so it only stands to reason that salvation would be for all. Paul said the same thing in other words, "In the same way that everyone dies in Adam, so also everyone will be given life in Christ" (1 Corinthians 15:22).

Universal salvation is mystery. But it is also revelation.[31] It is beyond explanation, but not beyond expectation. In fact, it is our greatest hope, that God is at work so that no one and nothing will perish, but that all shall come to salvation (2 Peter 3:9). All means all.

Prayer: God, the best news is that you love the whole world, and love wins. Amen!

Week Thirty, Day 3

Read 2 Corinthians 3:18

Years ago, Lewis Smedes wrote a book titled A Pretty Good Person. In it he said, "Pretty good is good enough."[32] There is wisdom and health in these words. They save us from a toxic spirituality of perfectionism—one that keeps us feeling restless and creates an image of God who is perpetually displeased with us.

Of course, there are things about ourselves we should not ignore, but our spiritual formation occurs best along the lines of moving "from one degree of glory to another" (NRSVue) as Paul put it, not from a "never enough" sense of ourselves. Satisfaction is not about pride or thinking we have "arrived. It is an oasis on the journey—a rest stop for the soul. It is an invitation from Christ himself, "Come by yourselves to a secluded place and rest for a while" (Mark 6:31). It's hearing Jesus say, "Good job." Pretty good is good enough.

Prayer: God, I'll do the best I can, and then rest, knowing it is good enough. Amen.

Week Thirty, Day 4

Read Matthew 20:1-16

We can always find someone who has worked longer and harder at something than we have. After being told "Don't be late" so often, it's difficult to get involved in something when we feel like we're latecomers.

But the fact is, we are rarely the first person God calls to do something. If nothing else, we come late to something simply because others have lived before us. But even setting history aside, we almost always become involved after others have done so.

Today's reading is important if we are to overcome a "what's the use?" way of thinking. Jesus's parable sends a clear message: it's not how long we work that matters; what matters is that we work. When God calls us to labor in a vineyard, the important thing is that we say yes. God pays the same wage to us all because it is not based on the depth or duration of our service, but on the fact that we went to work where and when God asked us to.

Prayer: God, when you call, I will not look at what others have done. I will see what I can do. Amen.

Week Thirty, Day 5

Read Acts 4:20

In scripture recognition and responsibility are linked. The phrase "if you see something, say something" communicates the biblical spirit. We see it in the words of Peter and John. It's further illustrated in the experiences of Mary in the garden (John 20:11-18), the couple on the road to Emmaus (Luke 24:13-35), and Rhoda (Acts 12:13-16). Indeed, it is the pattern of discipleship.

The message is clear: we must go and tell what we have seen and heard. This is what it means to be a witness. A sighting that does not become a story is not a seeing. "Come and see" is followed by "go and tell."

There is no one-size-fits-all way to do this. This story comes through our story. Truth is personified. It is the pattern of incarnation—Jesus's and ours: the word must become flesh. Revelation calls for a response.

Prayer: God, you show, and I will tell. Amen.

Week Thirty-one, Day 1

Read Matthew 6:5-13 and Luke 11:1-4

By all accounts, prayer is the chief means of grace. This is so for at least two reasons: prayer is our ultimate urge (to commune with God), and it is the supreme definition of faith (a relationship with God). Jesus highlighted the importance of prayer in the passages above. We will explore them in the next round of meditations.

Today we focus on the passage in Luke to make two introductory points: the praying Jesus is the greatest validation of prayer, and prayer can be taught. The disciples' hunger to pray came alive when they saw Jesus praying, and being their rabbi, he taught them to pray by giving them a pattern for it.

We call it the Lord's Prayer, but it is our prayer too. We pray it verbatim in private devotion and public worship as our recognition of its value. We "pray like this" by expressing the sentiments found in the prayer itself. We will look at those in the coming days.

Prayer: God, teach me to pray. It's what I want most to do. Amen.

Week Thirty-one, Day 2

Read Matthew 6:5 and Luke 11:2

On both occasions when Jesus spoke about prayer, he said, "*when* you pray," not "if you pray." The first thing we learn about prayer is that it is natural. We are made to pray. And we all pray.

Jesus's disciples were already praying because they were human and because they were Jews. Their humanity gave them the thirst for prayer (Psalm 42:1), their faith gave them the opportunities to pray (Psalm 119:164). When they asked Jesus to teach them to pray, they did not mean to start praying, but to improve their praying.

That's what we mean too. We do not need to be taught to start praying, but we all need to be helped to pray better. Indeed, we can be taught to pray better. Jesus's school of prayer begins here; the Lord's Prayer is the curriculum for praying better.

Prayer: God, I am made for prayer. Teach me to pray. Amen.

Week Thirty-one, Day 3

Read Matthew 6:9

We never pray alone. No matter when we pray, untold others are praying. But more, we do not pray in isolation, but rather as members of one human family. The word *our* is Jesus's teaching that we pray in community.

We need especially to see this. Too much religion today is privatized—a "me and God" spirituality. Jesus will not let us get by with that. The first word in the Lord's Prayer puts an end to this kind of thinking.

To pray in community is to hold the world in our heart, with a Bible in one hand and a newspaper in the other. Praying in community is also being moved into action. Like God, to see the world is to care for it in some way. Prayer gives us the vision and the compassion for living well. It's all in the word *our*.

Prayer: God, teach me to pray so that I can see the world as it is and care for it as I can. Amen.

Week Thirty-one, Day 4

Read Matthew 6:9 and Luke 11:2

We pray as family. "Father" is not about God's masculinity, it's about our affinity with one another. We are siblings. This intensifies the sense of community we looked at in the previous meditation. We are all God's children, and (as Robert Fulghum put it), we "hold hands and stick together."[33] We journey together through thick and thin.

"Father" also tells us about God's disposition toward us. Jesus used the word *abba* to describe God, the word a child would use for an earthly father—a term of affection based in trust and expressed in happiness. The Lord's Prayer begins with the note of joy.

"Father" says we are in a relationship, with one another and with God. We are kin, living together in love in the kingdom of God—the "kindom" of God.

Prayer: God, I rejoice to know I am your beloved child in your forever family. Amen.

Week Thirty-one, Day 5

Read Matthew 6:9

When Robert Browning wrote in his poem "Pippa Passes" that "God's in His heaven— / All's right with the world!" he was restating the phrase in the Lord's Prayer, "who is in heaven."

The phrase is not about God's location "out there somewhere" or a way of saying that God is distant, removed, or unconcerned. Rather, it is a way of saying that we are secure, we have nothing to fear. The connection between heaven and earth is reliable. The phrase means we can live confidently.

Our lives falter when we approach them tentatively. We cease to take risks and begin to play it safe. Security is the foundation for abundant living—the conviction that God is with us. The security in this phrase of the prayer extends to times of failure. Even when we get it wrong and head off in the wrong direction, we can always turn around, secure that in all things we are God's beloved.

Prayer: God I am secure in you. I will live confidently. Amen.

Week Thirty-two, Day 1

Read Matthew 6:9 and Luke 6:2

God's sovereignty is not meant to make us feel distant from God or afraid of God. But it is meant to inspire a spirit of reverence in us. That's what the phrase "hallowed be thy name" means. It does not mean we make God's name holy; it means that we recognize that it is.

In 1933, Albert Schweitzer wrote the book *Reverence for Life*. It was his testimony to the fact that reverence is the disposition that defines and directs the way we live. As the Lord's Prayer shows, reverence for God is the foundation upon which our reverence for everyone and everything else is built.

When we do not reverence the creation, it is a sign that we do not reverence the God who made it. Jesus teaches us to pray in a way that gets the center of our life straight, knowing that when it is, all that's on the circumference will be treated as holy too.

Prayer: God, I will start by reverencing you and let this root produce the fruit of reverence for everyone and everything else. Amen.

Week Thirty-two, Day 2

Read Matthew 6:10 and Luke 11:2

When Jesus told us to pray "thy kingdom come, thy will be done on earth as it is in heaven," he was teaching that prayer is a collaborative effort. John Wesley spoke similarly, "Without God, we cannot; without us, God will not."

In a real way, just as we reverence God (see the last meditation), God reverences us—by inviting us to pray as those who offer ourselves as cocreators with God in bringing the divine will to pass. This is what Paul had in mind when he urged us to offer ourselves to God as living sacrifices (Romans 12:1).

We are often the means through whom God works—instruments of God's peace, as St. Francis put it. When we ask God to do something, we must be ready to hear God say, "I will do it . . . through you."

Prayer: "God, what are you doing in the world today that I can help you with?"[34]

Week Thirty-two, Day 3

Read Matthew 6:11 and Luke 11:3

When Jesus told us to ask God for daily bread, he was drawing on at least two ideas from Judaism. The first was the provision of manna (Exodus 16:1-36). The second was the gift of God's love

(Psalm 90:14). Both were said to be given each morning. Manna feeds the body; love nourishes the soul. Both are our everyday nourishment.

In this phrase we are assured of God's total care for us, physically and spiritually. In God's provision there is no separation of body and soul or any hierarchy between them. In addition, "daily bread" is another way to live in the present moment. Each day is the means through which God cares for us.

This phrase saves us from two errors in life: first, looking for meaning in the past or future. And second, recognizing God's provision only in its "big" expressions. Instead, both errors are addressed here, and we are reminded that "now is the day of salvation" (2 Corinthians 6:2). In this phrase Jesus says, "Look for God here and now."

Prayer: God, I look for you in the present moment and in the amount that meets my current need. Amen.

Week Thirty-two, Day 4

Read Matthew 6:12 and Luke 11:4

Forgiveness is the only petition in the Lord's Prayer that Jesus commented on immediately after the prayer (Matthew 6:14). This is likely due to the fact that forgiveness is the hardest gift to receive and to give. The Lord's Prayer includes both, and assures us that each is possible.

God is more willing to forgive us than we are to ask to be forgiven. Interestingly, our ability to accept our forgiveness is linked to our willingness to forgive others. Think of it like taking a container out into the rain. The larger it is, the more water we can capture. Similarly, the larger our heart is to forgive others, the more fully we will be disposed to sense and accept God's forgiveness.

Forgiveness is not overlooking sin, it's overcoming it. Forgiveness is being set free. Jesus emphasized the forgiveness of sins in his ministry because he knew how much we long to be forgiven.

Prayer: God, I will enlarge my sense of your forgiveness of my sins by increasing my willingness to forgive others of theirs. Amen.

Week Thirty-two, Day 5

Read Matthew 6:13 and Luke 11:4

No phrase in the Lord's Prayer has caused more confusion than "lead us not into temptation." It does not seem like anything we would ever need to pray for, since it is not something God would ever do (James 1:13). But yet, there is the request. What's going on?

As it turns out, the problem is not theological, it's linguistic. "Lead us not into" is not the way we say things today. Instead, we would say, "lead us away from." And that's what the phrase means. Indeed, it is the very thing Paul says God does in the verse referenced above.

Jesus and James are saying the same thing. Jesus simply made the truth James described into a prayer we can pray, "God, lead me away from temptation." God is our Shepherd, and one thing shepherds do is lead their sheep away from danger. Every time we pray the Lord's Prayer, we are asking God to do the same for us.

Prayer: God, steer me away from danger. Amen.

Week Thirty-three, Day 1

Read Matthew 6:13

Being led away from temptation is protection. Deliverance from evil is rescue. We need both. Sometimes we don't have the sense or the will to heed the warnings or walk through the exits. Sometimes we don't wake up until we are already in a mess. What then?

We pray to be rescued. It's summed up in one word: *help!* Every parent has heard a child cry out for it. Every one of us has received a message from a friend asking for it. And what do we do? We come to their rescue.

Jesus says God does the same.

"Help!" is not predicated on deserving it, but only on needing it. There is a time and place for introspection, analysis, confession, and so on. "Help!" is not one of those times. God delivers us for one reason only: we need to be rescued. On our end of the dilemma, we have only one job: to ask for help. The sooner, the better.

Prayer: God, I realize there is a prayer for anytime I get in a mess: "Help!" You have given me the word to use because it is what you want to do. Thank you. Amen.

Week Thirty-three, Day 2

Read Matthew 16:13

It depends on which version of the Bible you are using as to whether or not the Lord's Prayer ends with "for thine is the kingdom, and the power, and the glory forever." Many scholars believe the phrase was added when the church began to use the prayer in public worship.

We will include it as a way to say a final thing about this prayer in particular, and about prayer in general. That is, prayer begins and ends in the heights of adoration. No matter what we say in prayer, we say it against the backdrop of God's majesty— God's reign, power, and glory. We end praying with confidence that we have addressed the Almighty.

These words are celebratory. In them we say, "You're the One!"—the One to whom we entrust our lives, in every respect, forever. We end our praying with the declaration that our times are in God's hands from beginning to end.

Prayer: God, it's all about you, and I am totally OK with that. Amen.

Week Thirty-three, Day 3

Read Matthew 6:5-6

Before leaving the Lord's Prayer, we learn more about it by looking at why Jesus gave it to us in the first place. Matthew and Luke set the prayer in two different contexts. In Matthew, the context is the difference between false and true religion.

One of the dangers of religion is that it gives us the platform for practicing our piety to impress others (Matthew 6:1). In the Sermon on the Mount, Jesus gave three examples of showy religion: altruism, fasting, and prayer. Showy prayer is characterized by two things: making it about public display, and making it wordy. Neither is bad as a means (i.e., public prayer is not bad and long prayers are not wrong), but when they become ends, prayer goes off the rails.

Together, these two things raise the question, "Why do we pray." Unless we can say it is to commune with God (Matthew 6:6), we need to take another look at our praying.

Prayer: God, cleanse me of false motives for praying, and center me anew in the true reason: to be with you. Amen.

Week Thirty-three, Day 4

Read Luke 11:1

It may well be that our longing to pray is our deepest desire, because our yearning to commune with God is at the heart of what it means to be made in the image of God. With our capacity for relationship in the imago Dei, we are moved to express it. And so, we pray.

As we do, we want to enrich our praying. We want to improve our prayer life. This yearning was in the hearts of Jesus's disciples. Every one of them had prayed before they approached him. They came to Jesus asking him to help them pray better. So they said, "Teach us to pray."

Our longing to pray, and pray better, can be increased by teaching. Prayer can be taught. We noted that days ago, but it bears repeating now. If that were not so, Jesus would have denied their request. But he didn't; he gave them the curriculum, the pattern. He taught them to "pray like this." Like the first disciples, we can be taught to pray; we can enrich our prayer life. The Lord's Prayer is our first class in Christ's school of prayer.

Prayer: God, teach me to pray. Amen.

Week Thirty-three, Day 5

Read 1 Thessalonians 5:17

Our look at the Lord's Prayer is not complete until we put it into its context: "pray continually." These are Paul's words but they communicate Jesus's sentiment and reflect his example. We do no greater harm to prayer in general or the Lord's Prayer in particular than to view it as an occasional practice.

Prayer is an abiding disposition. Prayer is more a life to be lived than words to be spoken—a life in which all we think, say, and do is in relation to God. Prayer is the singular center that defines multifaceted circumference of our lives. "Have I prayed about it?" is no peripheral question; it is the orienting and empowering one.

In any given moment, some dimension of the Lord's Prayer that we have looked at will be the activating attitude and agenda-setting action for how are to live in that situation. The Lord's Prayer is the air we breathe as we move through the days of our lives.

Prayer: God, I will make times for praying the Lord's Prayer. But more, I will make the Lord's prayer the spirit in which I live my times. Amen.

Week Thirty-four, Day 1

Read 2 Corinthians 5:1

The focus of our faith is not heaven, but the Bible speaks enough about heaven to assure us it is there. We live here and now, but we do so with confidence that when this life is over, it's not the end.

In fact, Paul's imagery calls this life a tent, but when it comes to life in heaven, he says it's a house that is not handmade. It's his way of showing that life after death is more substantial than life before death.

Scripture leaves heaven in the context of mystery, not because God doesn't want us to know about it, but rather because it is indescribable in words we could understand. We can no more grasp what heaven is than a baby in the womb can grasp what earth is. So, the Bible just says, "It's real." And Paul lets us know it's better than the life we're living now.

Prayer: God, I rest in the confidence that heaven is real. That's good enough for me. Amen.

Week Thirty-four, Day 2

Read Genesis 1:2

We know that God is not identified by gender, but our understanding of God has been diminished by references to God as "him." Thankfully, some of the saints (most notably Julian of Norwich) have helped us see God's feminine side, providing us with the Father/Mother God. We continue to benefit from others today who are helping us see the fullness of God.

But the fact is, the feminine dimensions of God are in the Bible. In fact, the first reference—the verse above—is feminine; God is described as hovering over creation, which is what a mother bird does over her chicks in the nest.

From there, scripture goes on to include feminine metaphors for God—for example, Deuteronomy 32:18; Psalm 22:10; 131:2; Isaiah 42:14; 49:15; Hosea 11:3; 13:8; Matthew 23:37; and Luke 15:8.

Our faith is enriched as our concept of God is expanded, when we bring masculinity and femininity together.

Prayer: I thank you for giving me Father/Mother love. Amen.

Week Thirty-four, Day 3

Read Acts 5:29

Everybody gives allegiance to something. The apostles announced that they gave theirs to God. They knew that we live from the center, that we live from the heart (Matthew 15:19).[35]

In the context of today's reading, the apostles' choice gave them courage to bear witness and endure opposition. Obedience provides the foundation for our faith. It gave them a place to stand when they were persecuted.

Our center is the reference point that defines and arranges the many points on the circumference of our lives. We cannot wait until the heat's on to figure out what that center is. We must nail it down in advance of the storms. If we do, we will be ready to live our faith when it's under fire.

Prayer: God, you are my center, the source of my obedience in every other area of my life. Amen.

Week Thirty-four, Day 4

Read Luke 3:21-22

The word *trinity* does not appear in the New Testament, but the idea does. In fact, it comes up in Jesus's baptism: the Father speaks, the Son is baptized, and the Spirit descends. In every respect this is a mysterious passage, but it set the trajectory for Jesus's ministry. In that ministry he repeatedly spoke of both his relationship with the Father and the Spirit.

Over the centuries, Christians have used many analogies to talk about the Trinity. All fall short of a complete explanation. So, what do we do with the Trinity? We affirm it without understanding it, like we do with many other things in life.

"I believe" is not a sign that we have grasped something as much as it is indication that we have been grasped by it. "I believe" is an indication of our conviction, not our comprehension. When we confess our faith in the Trinity, we are saying, "What a wonderful God we have."

Prayer: God, I will never understand you, but I will ever adore you. Amen.

Week Thirty-four, Day 5

Read Ephesians 2:14-16

The dividing wall went up in Eden; it came down on the cross. By the time Paul wrote to the Ephesians, the wall was described as being between Jews and Gentiles, which simply meant between everybody.

Thousands of years later, we erect walls to separate us from one another. We build racial, economic, political, sexual, educational, and border walls—to name a few. We are a fragmented people. And the rough edges and sharp points of our separations are causing great harm.

Of all the things we can say about the life and work of Jesus, there is none more needed and urgent than this: he came to remove the dividing walls. Wherever we see people building tangible or ideological walls, we know they are not doing the work of Christ. In turn, we know we are doing his work when we remove walls that divide and advocate for the common good.

Prayer: God, thank you for the work of Christ to remove walls. I will join him in that effort. Amen.

Week Thirty-five, Day 1

Read Exodus 23:9

From the time when God first established the covenant with the Israelites, the message has been clear, "Don't oppress an immigrant." Yet too much of the world does the exact opposite. In doing so we work in opposition to God's will.

We can only oppress people when we have forgotten we are siblings in the human family. We can only oppress people when we have separated ourselves from them by means of "othering" and viewing them as "less than" we are. We can only oppress others when we give them labels rather than names.

"Don't oppress an immigrant" is rooted in the enacted remembrance that we are one with everyone we meet. God's will is for unity. God's work is for unification, and we are the instruments God uses to accomplish it. Caring for immigrants is a sign that we do not see anyone as an "outsider," but as a fellow human being moving from one place to another.

Prayer: God give me the desire to live my life saying "Welcome" rather than "Get out." Amen.

Week Thirty-five, Day 2

Read 1 Corinthians 12:26

The Bible teaches a principle we have all but forgotten today: interbeing. It is more than sympathy (feeling for) or empathy (feeling with). It is identity (feeling as). Jesus spoke of the same thing when he told us to love our neighbors "as ourselves."

Our predecessors in faith were much better at this than we are. The recognized a unity of being that we have lost in our sense of separation. We have largely lost an organic understanding of life—where things interrelate for a common good—replacing it with a mechanical view where things are parts operating independently of one another.

The healing of the world and the cessation of harm we are doing to one another require the view of life that Paul described. Not until another's pain is our pain will we move from brokenness to wholeness. "I feel your pain" is a step toward the goal, but even that awaits the time when we say, "I hurt with your pain."

Prayer: God, move me past sympathy and empathy into identity. Amen.

Week Thirty-five, Day 3

Read Deuteronomy 30:19

There are many things beyond our control. When that's the case, we do well to pray these words of the Serenity Prayer, "to accept the things we cannot change." But we do so going on to pray the next phrase, "to change the things I can," and always praying for "the wisdom to know the difference."

In the context of choice, Moses exhorted the Israelites to "choose life." It was God's invitation extended through Moses's words, an invitation that required intention. We must accept the invitation, respond to it, and enact it.

Life is not automatic; existence is. Everyone is alive, but not everyone is "living" in the biblical sense of the word. We must choose life. Our choice is the key that opens the door to invigoration—to abundant living. God's invitation is always extended, and offered to all.

Prayer: God, I receive your invitation, with your RSVP included in it. And so, I respond—I choose life! Amen.

Week Thirty-five, Day 4

Read Psalm 62:5-6

At the Abbey of Gethsemani in Kentucky, two words are chiseled in stone near the entrance: "God Alone." In the monastic tradition it's the summary of the vocation of monks and nuns.[36] But what does it mean?

The words do not mean God "only," for a visit to a monastery or convent reveals them to be places of multiple activities that integrate worship and work. Prayer and productivity are blended together. The words mean God "ultimately"—God with no rivals—or God at the center, with everything lived in reference to God.

When you talk to monks and nuns about this, they see "God Alone" as the summary commitment that everyone should make, not just those living a cloistered life. All of us are meant to reference every aspect of our life in relation to God. The "God Alone" life is life as God intends it to be.

Prayer: God, with you at the center of my life, everything on the circumference finds its place and purpose. Amen.

Week Thirty-five, Day 5

Read Luke 12:48

These words of Jesus should not be read as if they are a burdensome duty, but rather as words of blessed delight. They are words inviting us to live generously.

Trees do not grow their fruit begrudgingly. They bear it in abundance. Sunrises and sunsets do not scrimp on their beauty. They bespangle the horizon. Similarly, the blessings we receive are "seeds" not meant for storing on a shelf, but rather intended to be sown into soil.

One of the signs of sin is stinginess, living with a scarcity mindset more intent upon taking from life rather than giving to it. An extraction economy is destroying us. God's call is to create ways and means that enrich people and the planet. Jesus's words are reminders that we are the instruments through whom the blessings of God get dispersed. If we have a servant's heart, we rejoice in having the opportunity to be cocreators with God.

Prayer: God, I understand that what you give me is not meant to stay with me, but rather flow beyond me to enhance the common good. Amen.

Week Thirty-six, Day 1

Read Luke 15:11-24

Sometimes we come upon people who believe they have wandered so far away from God that they would no longer be welcome back home. We may have felt that way ourselves. But it's not true. Jesus told this parable to give us the real message.

And it's this: the light is always shining on the front porch of God's house. Day or night we are welcome home. The story is not contingent on God; it hinges on us. The pivot, the thing that turns life around and heads it in the right direction is when we say, "I will get up and go to my father" (15:18).

That's it? Yes . . . that's it. Transformation does not require groveling; it's going home. History contains two thousand years of testimonies to this truth. We don't need to wonder, worry, or wait. All we have to do is get up and go.

Prayer: God, I understand that the light of your love is always shining for me. I am heading toward that light! Amen.

Week Thirty-six, Day 2

Read Psalm 142:5

The song "The Gambler" has the lyric "You've got to know when to hold 'em, know when to fold 'em." David was folding 'em. He was hiding from Saul in a cave (1 Samuel 24:3-4). In the Christian tradition the "cave of the heart" has become a symbol of how we think about God as our refuge, our hiding place.

It is important to see that the spiritual life includes hiding. Sometimes life is too much to handle. Stress too much to relieve. Pain too much to bear. Obstacles too great to overcome. Problems too great to solve. Grief too great to resolve.

In such times we are wise to hide out and hunker down. Bravado is not always the action. In fact, it can be foolish. Going into the cave creates space to think and pray, test and recoup. Psalm 142 shows David doing both. And it was in the cave where he found the next steps he needed to take to defeat Saul. We too sometimes find our way forward by seeking refuge.

Prayer: God, you are my hiding place. In you I find relief and renewal. Amen.

Week Thirty-six, Day 3

Read John 12:32

It's impossible to think about the cross without also seeing it as God's universal solution to the problem of sin. Jesus's words start the ball rolling. It continues to roll in the rest of the New Testament, picking up speed as it does so.[37]

Before 100 CE, the early Christians were convinced that Jesus died for all (Hebrews 7:27; 10:10), and that in Christ all shall be made alive (1 Corinthians 15:22), an aliveness that extends redemption to the entire creation (Romans 8:19-21).

We cannot have this vision without believing it will happen. Something this wonderful cannot fail to occur. God, who authored the vision, will bring it to pass (Ephesians 1:9-10). We are beneficiaries of amazing grace which, in the fullness of time, will "draw all people" (John 12:32 NRSVue) to God.

Prayer: God, this is too much for me to understand, but not too much for me to celebrate. I do! Amen.

Week Thirty-six, Day 4

Read Isaiah 43:19

God is present and active in creation all the time. We name this when we say God is our Sustainer. Ongoing involvement with everyone and everything is one way God is with us. But there are also times when God does a "new thing." Isaiah saw his day as such a time, and history teaches us that they come around every five hundred years or so.

We are living in such a time. Variously called an Axial Age, a New Pentecost, a New Reformation, another Great Awakening, or something similar, it is a pivotal period. It is a time of disorder as the old passes away and the new comes (2 Corinthians 5:17). It includes those who resist the change and those who facilitate it.

God calls us to be cocreators in such times, to be "instruments of God's peace" to use St. Francis's words. This is so important that we will continue the idea in tomorrow's meditation.

Prayer: God, I rejoice in the new thing you are doing. I offer myself to be one through whom you can work to bring it to pass. Amen.

Week Thirty-six, Day 5

Read Acts 15:1-17

The first Christians discerned that they were living in a time when God was once again doing a new thing. This time it was the addition of Gentiles into the Christian community, not just converts from Judaism. Inviting both Jews and Gentiles to follow Jesus was the church's way of saying that everyone is included.

Between then and now the church has divided more often than it has come together. And sadly today, some segments of Christianity embrace exclusion more than inclusion.

The "new thing" God is doing is the restoration of the earliest vision of the church: inclusion. We are called to honor the work of Jesus (John 12:32 and Colossians 1:20) and the discernment of the first Christians (Galatians 3:28). In our day this is particularly focused on the full inclusion of women, non-white people, and LGBTQ+ people in the church's offices and ministries. God's new thing today is to live fully into the truth that "Christ is all and in all" (Colossians 3:11 NRSVue).

Prayer: God, use me to help you bring to pass the restoration of oneness in the church and world. Amen.

~·~

Week Thirty-seven, Day 1

Read Exodus 20:1-17

We want to live well. The Ten Commandments are God's instructions for doing so. They were not given, as some think, as a list of rules and regulations with a negative ("thou shalt not") or punitive intent. They were the ways God established for the Israelites to prosper when they entered the promised land. We will explore them this way.

The people were on the brink of living as never before. They had been slaves; soon they would be free. They had known scarcity; soon they would experience abundance. They had suffered, but soon they would be blessed in all sorts of ways. They needed to know how to live well in their new surroundings.

We are never more vulnerable than when we are secure and thriving. Temptations tumble in to lure us (personally and collectively) to abandon holiness. We need guidance in order to live faithfully. The Ten Commandments are God's teaching for doing that.

Prayer: God, I open myself to your instructions for living well. Amen.

Week Thirty-seven, Day 2

Read Exodus 20:1-7

We live well when we keep God central and give God our reverence and devotion. That's what the first three commandments are about. It's what the Bible and the Christian tradition mean by "living for God alone." Idolatry and irreverence prevent us from doing that.

Idolatry is putting anything in the center of our lives other than God. Idolatry is misplaced allegiance, which so easily turns into serving and worshipping false gods. But there's more. Idolatry in our hearts produces injustice in lives. That's the message running through the Prophets (e.g., Jeremiah 2:13). If our inner life toward God is not what it should be, our outer life toward others will not be either.

Irreverence is the attitude that runs through idolatry. It is the disposition of life that ends up ruining our will to love and our ability to do so. So the first two commandments tell us to keep God central. Everything turns on whether or not we do this.

Prayer: God, my heart is your home, not just as a guest, but as the owner. Amen.

Week Thirty-seven, Day 3

Read Exodus 20:8-11

The first three commandments establish the priority that helps us live well: keeping God central. The fourth commandment establishes the pattern for doing so: honoring the sabbath.

Like each of the Ten Commandments, this one points beyond itself to something larger. In this case, the focus on one day is the way we see every day in perspective. All seven days are mentioned, providing the rhythm of life God wants for us: working and resting.

In our day, the sabbath principle has been all but lost in the 24/7 world that never sleeps and promotes sleep deprivation in us. Succumbing to freneticism, we experience hurry sickness. The sabbath is a callback to the rhythm of working and resting. It is the way of wellness. And as we live into the pattern, we find that the centrality of God is manifested in our worship and in our work.

Prayer: God, I want my heart to beat in rhythm with yours: working and resting. Amen.

Week Thirty-seven, Day 4

Read Exodus 20:12

When we come to the fifth commandment, we see the importance God places on the family. We are to honor our parents.

This command fits into the perspectives of the times—that second only to the reverencing of God is respecting our parents.

Honoring clearly means holding them in high esteem, but it is an act that goes beyond words to providing for them. Parents uncared for was a public witness to the failure of children to honor them. In short, honoring parents is a comprehensive act—a thought, word, and deed expression of love.

This commandment assumed that our parents are honorable. Honoring is not artificial. It is not gushing. It is not ignoring parental sin when it's there. If it is, honoring means doing no harm toward our parents, while at the same time not subjecting ourselves to their harm.

The promise of long life meant to show that honoring is healthy (versus being consumed by selfishness or anger). Honoring parents is honoring life.

Prayer: God, I will honor those who gave me life. Amen.

Week Thirty-seven, Day 5

Read Exodus 20:13

In a real sense, the Ten Commandments follow the flow of the opening chapters of the Bible, restoring through the covenant what was lost in the fall: reverence for God and others.

This commandment puts us back in the beginning of Genesis 4, where Cain killed Abel. Murder is wrong both because it takes another's life, and also because it ends up taking our life also as we give way to jealousy, animosity, and envy. Abel was dead, but Cain was too. There's more than one way to die.

Reverence for life is at the heart of the Judeo-Christian religion, indeed of all religions. Life is sacred, and no one has the right to bring another's life to an end.

Furthermore, the commandment is generic, so that it can easily be applied to other sentient beings, not just humans. In every world religion, respect for life is paramount, a respect that is proactive in the doing of good to all.

Prayer: God, I will not harm what you have made. Amen.

⇜⇝

Week Thirty-eight, Day 1

Read Exodus 20:14

We are only as good as the commitments we make. This commandment points to that, using the vows people make to each other in marriage to illustrate the fidelity that should characterize all our relationships.

Adultery is the literal act that violates the most sacred relationship God could create: marriage. But the word also serves as a larger metaphor for failing to prove that we mean what we say. It is, at least in the beginning, using words that are not confirmed in deeds. Almost always, adultery is done in secrecy. Adultery is the mark that we cannot be trusted. When that is the case in any area of life, it is probably true in other areas too.

That's why the term "one flesh" is used in the Bible for the relationships God wants us to have. It is not a physical or sexual term as its multiple uses reveal. It is a deep bond of trustworthiness, what we call "being joined at the hip." From ancient times until know, our character is seen in our conduct. As Jesus said, we are known by our fruits.

Prayer: God, I will prove my faithfulness through my actions. Amen.

Week Thirty-eight, Day 2

Read Exodus 20:15

God intends for us to accept what we have and to respect what others have. It does not mean that we cease trying to improve our lives, but it does mean that we do not seek to do so at another's expense.

Stealing is thievery, living with a "what's yours is mine, I'll take it" philosophy of life. It is the way the robbers thought as they mugged the traveler in Jesus's parable of the good Samaritan (Luke 10:25-37). It is domination, exploitation; it is greed enacted.

The gaps among people groups are created and sustained by stealing. The depletion of the earth is generated and increased by stealing. Stealing is treating sentient beings as objects to be possessed rather than cared for. And God forbids it.

Instead, we are meant to live in ways that say, "what's mine is yours, I'll share it." It's what made the Samaritan good, and what makes us good too.

Prayer: God, I will not steal from other people and things; I will serve them. Amen.

Week Thirty-eight, Day 3

Read Exodus 20:16

Life is only as genuine as it is true. Falsehood always diminishes us and others. The ninth commandment uses "neighbor" language to teach this truth. It's the word used elsewhere in scripture—the word that keeps the tone loving and the audience wide.[38]

The fallen-world narrative exists on untruth, in whole or in part. Sin tells the story to make the sinners look good. National histories are sanitized to hide racism, oppression, and exploitation. Individual histories are told so as to make the person look superhuman, even messianic. But more, false witnessing creates "others" who are "less than." It shuns and shames. It dominates and subjugates, excludes and separates.

God says no to lying. God is true (singular, authentic, and trustworthy), and we are made and meant to be so too.

Prayer: God, I will be true, inside and out in every way. Amen.

Week Thirty-eight, Day 4

Read Exodus 20:17

The Ten Commandments begin and end in the heart. They have to do with wrong desire—wrong desire with respect to God, and now in the final commandment, wrong desire with respect to other people and things. The sins in between are outward signs of an inner problem: heart disease.

The Ten Commandments are constructed so that we remember to keep our inner life in good shape, both in relation to God and others. The Ten Commandments are the love foundation later made even more specific in the Law (Deuteronomy 6:5; Leviticus 19:18), in the teaching of Jesus (Matthew 22:34-40), and in the rest of the New Testament (e.g., 1 Corinthians 13; 1 John 3:13–5:5).

God did not give the Ten Commandments primarily to show us how not to sin, but rather to show us how to love. Sin is always in some way a failure to love. As the Jews journeyed from Egypt toward the promised land, God had one intention: to make them loving toward themselves and everyone/everything else. The Ten Commandments were the first move in that direction.

Prayer: God, move my heart to love. Amen.

Week Thirty-eight, Day 5

Read Exodus 20:1-17

We end these meditations on the Ten Commandments pointing to a major misunderstanding between the Old and New Testaments of the Bible. It's been alleged that the Old Testament is about law, and the New Testament is about love. But that's wrong. The whole Bible is about love. It's the singular message of scripture.

The Ten Commandments put love at the heart of the Law. In fact, when law loses its love essence, it turns into legalism, with pride and judgmentalism arising soon afterward. That's what had happened to the Law in Jesus's day, so he said he came to restore the Law to what God intended for it to be. He used the word *fulfill* to describe what he was doing (Matthew 5:17). He was refilling (filling full) the Law of what it had been drained of: love.

Love is at the core of law, not surprisingly because God is love. The covenant is the means by which we enact love. The Jews of the exodus were in God's school of love, and so are we. Where God's will is done, love defines the moment and leads the way from our "egypts" to the "promised land."

Prayer: God, teach me to love. Amen.

❧❧

Week Thirty-nine, Day 1

Read Romans 2:13-16

Before the Ten Commandments were written in stone, God wrote them (indeed, all the Law) on the hearts of people. Paul's reference to the Gentiles was his way of saying "everyone." And as

Paul also noted, the purpose of the Law was not that it be heard, but that it be enacted.

From the time of creation until now we have never been without the law. God's will has been plain since time began. What ebbs and flows is obedience, not revelation. The new covenant was given to the world through Christ to get us back to "heart religion" (Hebrews 8:10).

That's why what we saw in the Ten Commandments (the law of the love of God and neighbor) runs through the rest of the Bible. It is carried in the heart from generation to generation.

We can have the law in stone (in print) and still fail to live by it. Outward religion is not a guarantee of inward reality. But when God's way is in our hearts, disobedience is far less likely. The God-human "heart connection" offers us more than words in stone ever can.

Prayer: God, inscribe your will on my heart. Amen.

Week Thirty-nine, Day 2

Read 1 John 5:3

The notion that God issued commands to cramp our style has been around for a long time. From time to time someone will still say, "I don't want to have anything with 'thou shalt not' religion." The idea that God's commands are burdensome is still around.

That's why it is important to read today's verse and see the first Christians did not see it that way. They did not view obedience negatively. Why? Because they understood that love was the motive for God giving the Law in the first place. The covenant gives us wings, it does not put us in a cage.

There is negative, burdensome law. We call it legalism. It is law that's censorious and judgmental. Jesus saw it in his day and called it out (Matthew 23:4). Legalism still exists. We have to keep calling it out. We do it like Jesus and the first Christians did—by declaring that love is the essence of God's commands. They are meant to help us thrive. Where God's laws are present and active, love prevails.

Prayer: God, I gladly obey your commands because they are signs of your love, and in keeping them, I live. Amen.

Week Thirty-nine, Day 3

Read Sirach 1:26

The aim of the spiritual life is not knowledge, it's wisdom. Wisdom is the fruit of lived experience. In becoming wise we live our way into a new way of thinking. Obedience is the way to wisdom.

Behavior is the bridge into truth, for in the biblical sense truth is not a concept as much as it is the result of putting God's will into action. Concepts can be correct, but they become true when they have been proven to be so in everyday living.

The Wisdom Tradition in the Bible is our guide because it schools us in ethical living, compassionate living, and joyful living. Wisdom is a person (a woman) in scripture to show it is behavior, not just belief. Jesus was a Wisdom teacher (a sage) because his aim was living faith, not dead orthodoxy. Even more, he was the Wisdom of God incarnate (1 Corinthians 1:24) to reveal that God's will is to be done "on earth as it is in heaven."

God's commands are part of the Wisdom Tradition because they call us to perform faith, not just profess it.

Prayer: God, I will live my way into wisdom. Amen.

Week Thirty-nine, Day 4

Read Matthew 5:21-48

The commandments were written in stone, but they are not set in stone. They are not fixed, but fluid. Jesus showed us this six times in the Sermon on the Mount, saying, "You have heard that it was said. . . . But I say. . . ."

In doing this, he was illustrating that the commandments of God are to be understood in the context of the time in which they are applied. The commandments were lived differently in the desert than they were in the nation. Jesus took five commandments and expanded them to fit the situation of his hearers.[39]

We must do the same. The content of God's truth must be poured into the containers of the times in which we live. This is not easy, but it is necessary.

Prayer: God, I accept your commands and my need to apply them to life as I live it today. Amen.

Week Thirty-nine, Day 5

Read John 15:12

Jesus knew that God's commands could be misinterpreted. They not only needed to be taught; they needed to be illustrated. So, he added the phrase "as I have loved you" to his affirmation of God's commands. The disciples were able to say "We get it because we've seen it."

These meditations were written during a mass exodus of people out of institutional religion (we call them "Dones"), and a growing number of others not seeking God through institutional means (we call them "Nones"). They are leaving and staying away because they have heard the message, but they have not seen it lived by the messengers. Religions of words without deeds do not attract people, and they cannot keep them.

Jesus knew this, so he was careful to instruct his disciples in faith that is professed and performed, believed and behaved. This was Jesus's version of "show-and-tell," and the combination is how the gospel comes alive.

Prayer: God, I will do what Jesus told us to do: to live what we learn. Amen.

❧

Week Forty, Day 1

Read Colossians 3:14

From the Christian vantage point, the spiritual life is life in Christ, not only the incarnate Christ in Jesus, but the excarnate Christ of the cosmos—the Christ of time and eternity. This was early Christianity's testimony, and Paul declared it with laser-beam focus in his Letter to the Colossians.

But what kind of life is it? Paul made that clear too, it is the life of love. The title of this book, *Coming Alive,* is an exhortation to love. Every meditation in this book is written directly or indirectly to advance the life of love. But as we head into the homestretch of our year-long reading and reflecting on scripture, the remainder of the meditations will be about love.

The mountain range of revelation has observable "love peaks." We will hike through them between now and the end of this book. We do this in the spirit of Paul, who told us above all else to put on love.

Prayer: God, I enroll in your School of Love. Amen.

Week Forty, Day 2

Read John 3:16

Our pursuit of love is a response to having been previously loved. Our love is a response to God's love. "We love because God first loved us" (1 John 4:19).

And what a love it is! Love for the whole world. There's no way we can believe we're not included. God's expression of love knows no bounds and has no exceptions.

There are many people who have not been loved by others, but there is no one who's been unloved by God. There are many who do not feel loved, but the feeling does not come from God. We are God's beloved. Period. We are loved. Full stop.

The myriad of passages that tell us more about love are all built on the foundation of God's love. God is love. God loves. God loves us. God loves everyone.

Prayer: God, you love me . . . completely and all the time. Amen.

Week Forty, Day 3

Psalm 31:7

Ask married couples what love means to them, and they will likely describe it in terms of friendship and faithfulness. They may include other things, but they name those two as a way of saying that what love means, when all is said and done, is relationship and reliability.

That's the essence of *hesed*. It's the combination of God's kindness and loyalty. The thing that makes the relationship most enjoyable is that it is secure. The word *Immanuel* (God with us) is one way we describe it, and it not only means God's presence in our lives but also God's support of us.

David wrote that God's *hesed* gave him great joy and moved him to celebration. This was his way of saying he wanted to show his love for God in the ways God had shown it to him. The wonderful thing about a Great Love is that it makes us great lovers.

Prayer: God, I receive your love with gratitude, and I return it with joy. Amen.

Week Forty, Day 4

Read 1 John 3:1

The kind of love God shows us is agape. The first Christians chose this Greek word for love, among other options, to describe the essence of God's love for us.

This is the word that roots love in the giver, not the receiver—that is, God loves us without first deciding whether we deserve it or not. It is love based in grace, not merit. There is no better news than this because it means we are God's beloved children all the time, no matter what. God's love never ends, and it is unconditional.

As we will see later when we spend more time in 1 John, this kind of love can be in us too, in the same way that the Old Testament reveals *hesed* to be a love we can express. The way of love begins, continues, and ends in God. But along the way it can be in us and be given out by us.

Prayer: God, we are in a Lover-beloved relationship. Thank you! Teach me how to manifest your love in all my relationships. Amen.

Week Forty, Day 5

Read 1 Corinthians 14:1

Trails have markers to help us know we are on the right path and not sidetracked. The "*hesed*/agape" marker is the way we know we are on the trail God wills for us.

Markers are placed on the trail before we ever get there. Our task is to look for them and follow where they lead us. In the life of love, we do not create the love, but we do walk in the manner it lays out for us.

We make love our aim. That is, we aim to live our lives as love-defined and love-directed people. Our aim is to live our lives on this planet as those who love—God, others, and ourselves. We look to the biblical markers to keep us on the path. In the next round of meditations, we take our hike through scripture on the Love Trail, paying particular attention to some of the peaks we see along the way.

Prayer: God, you have gone ahead of me to lay out the trail you want me to follow. It's the Love Trail marked by the "*hesed*/agape" signs. Off we go! Amen.

Week Forty-one, Day 1

Read Genesis 1:1–2:4a

The Love Trail begins with creation. Creation for God is an act of love. It is the nature of love to create. Parents know this. Artists do too. Creation is an outward action that reveals an inward heart. Creation is an act of love because God is love.

We hike through the mountain range of love with this primal reality accompanying us every step of the way. In the first creation story, we see love in God's creation of Adam and Eve in the divine image, and God's companionship with them. Everything is relational, and it is a relationship of love.

What began in creation continues on every page of scripture. It doesn't matter where in the Bible we are reading. Whenever we encounter God, it is an encounter with love. Sometimes it is convicting love, but it is always about love. Every step is an arrival into love, a step toward a homecoming in God's house of love. The light is on right now!

Prayer: God, I walk with you in love. Amen.

Week Forty-one, Day 2

Read Genesis 9:1-17

The next mountain peak on the Love Trail is the covenant. God did not create the cosmos and then walk away from it. To the contrary, God made promises to everyone and everything. That fact is repeated over and over in the passage.

The word for these promises is panentheism, a word that means God is in all that is made. The Creator-creation distinction is in place, but nothing and no one is disconnected from God. The covenant is the outward sign of the inward reality.

The covenant is the sign of God's love to everyone and everything. It is variously referred to as "steadfast love," "faithful love," everlasting love," "loyal love." The hymn writer called it the "love that will not let [us] go." Love is the basis of our relationship with God. It is our confidence and our hope.

Prayer: God, thank you for promising to love us always. Amen.

Week Forty-one, Day 3

Read Deuteronomy 6:4 and Leviticus 19:18

Love is not only implicit in the covenant, it is also explicit. Jesus pulled up the specific texts when he took the two verses in today's reading and called them the two Great Commandments. And then, he went a step further. He said that all the other commandments depend on these two (Matthew 22:40).

In teaching this he was saying that every single law is related to love—either the love of God or neighbor. Worship is the sign of our commitment to the first commandment; neighborliness is the sign of our obedience to the second.

In graphics, a vertical and horizontal line come together at a point called a nexus. In the spiritual life, love is the nexus. The love of God and the love of neighbor come together in us! We live from the heart (Proverbs 4:23). It is the life of love.

Prayer: God, I offer my heart as a meeting place for the vertical and horizontal lines of love. Amen.

Week Forty-one, Day 4

Read Psalm 121

The Love Trail is further experienced in Communion. The psalmist called it lifting our eyes to the hills and finding God present to help us.

The idea here is that God-of-the-Mountain is not "up there, somewhere." God is with us, observing us and interacting with us. It's God knowledgeable of and involved in our lives. We see it throughout the Bible, where God knows, sees, cares, and acts (e.g., Exodus 3).

The path of our life runs through the mountain range of God's love. At any point on the journey, all we have to do is lift up our eyes, and we will see God present and active with us. God is alert to our needs. God is our protector, keeping watch over us day and night, shading us from the blistering sun of evil, in all our comings and goings. The Love Trail is one on which we experience God's comprehensive care.

Prayer: God, wherever I look, you are there. Thank you. Amen.

Week Forty-one, Day 5

Read Isaiah 40:1-5

The Love Trail is one of comfort. We gathered as much in reading Psalm 121 yesterday, but today, Isaiah zeroes in on the message. His words are the theme of the second segment of the book (chapters 40–55).

Comfort is one of the "big ideas" in the Bible. It includes the immediate idea we have about it—the idea of being comforted (held close and cared for) in our times of need. But the word is not one that leaves us in our current state. To be comforted is to be strengthened, renewed, and given hope. Comfort is God's act of restoring us and moving us in the right direction. In the prophetic era, comfort was the return of the Israelites from exile.

The Love Trail is the road of life, the long and winding road that leads us home. But this is not returning to the status quo. It is an entrance into a "new normal"—what the Bible calls the new creation. God's comfort redefines life in terms of the kingdom of God.

Prayer: God, I seek your comfort as the gift you give to make me all you have in mind and all I want to be. Amen.

Week Forty-two, Day 1

Read John 1:14

The Love Trail leads us to Jesus, the "Everest" of love—the Word made flesh. The excarnate Christ of eternity became the incarnate Christ in time. Everything the Bible says about love is seen in him. And so, John says, we behold his glory.

There are a lot of debates about love today—whom to live, how to love, and so on. Even Christians are not in complete agreement about these things.

We go a long way in learning to love by looking at Jesus and then following him—that is, letting him lead us into becoming those who love God, others, and ourselves. In him we see love, and from him we receive power to love. It is the example and empowerment of love that is radical—that is universal and inclusive. The witness and message of Jesus is clear: "Live in love."

Prayer: God, I not only need to know about love, I need to see it. I do! In Jesus. Thank you. Amen.

Week Forty-two, Day 2

Read 1 Corinthians 14:1

The Love Trail winds past the mountain peak we call the church, whose purpose is to love. But as soon as we say this, we must hasten to say we do not mean "church" in the institutional sense. We mean it in its essential meaning: people called by God to live the life of love. The church is organic, not organizational, in its essence.

This does not mean we ignore the institutional church or despise it. It means we distinguish between church as people and church as institution, recognizing the two overlap but also realizing that the wineskin is not the wine. And so, we join with Christians over the centuries who ask God to confirm the church where it is right and correct it where it is wrong.

The difference is discerned through the lens of love. Where the church is the church as people (that is, loving), we commend it. Where the church as institution is unloving, we critique it and seek to restore it. In this way, the church becomes an entity that edifies us, but never one to which we sell our souls.

Prayer: God, I recognize the church, but I worship you. Amen.

Week Forty-two, Day 3

Read Acts 3:21; 1 Corinthians 15:22; and Ephesians 1:9-10

The Love Trail through the Bible ends at the mountain peak where time moves into eternity. And standing before it, we gaze on the final triumph of love. Christ has reconciled all things to God, things in heaven and things on earth (Colossians 1:20).

The Bible does not go into detail about how this happens. It only says that it will happen. The cross is the means of the cosmic atonement. This is the Bible's way of saying that our salvation is an accomplished fact—one that is now in motion until the time when every knee will bow and every tongue confess that Jesus Christ is Lord (Philippians 2:11).

The revelation of love in scripture is summed up in two words: love wins.[40] When we remember that God is love, how could it be any other way?

Prayer: God, I am yours now, and will be so eternally. Amen.

Week Forty-two, Day 4

Read John 13:1

Three days ago, we looked at Christ as the high peak in a theology of love. We reminded ourselves that we are called to love like Jesus. But what does that mean? What did Jesus himself show us about love and tell us about it? We turn to that in this next round of meditations.

The fact is, there's more to learn about love from Jesus than we have time and space to cover. He spoke about love nearly seventy times, and his loving acts increase that number. In our look at Jesus, we will explore selected actions and teachings as a way of turning the vague mantra "love like Jesus" into specifics.

Today we see the big picture. Jesus loved his disciples, and he loved them from start to finish. It's a good thing to receive acts of love from family, friends, and even strangers. But more than that is when such people love us all the time, from beginning to end, no matter what. When we have people like that in our lives, we are blessed indeed. Jesus is that kind of person. "What a friend we have in Jesus!"

Prayer: God, to be loved by Jesus, day in and day out is a great blessing. I receive it. Amen.

Week Forty-two, Day 5

Read John 15:13

Yesterday's meditation focused on the length and duration of Jesus's love. Today, we turn to the depth and extent of his love. He loves us so much that he gave his life for us. We call it atonement.

Unfortunately, Jesus's death has been falsely interpreted as the appeasement of God's anger. But Jesus did not go to the cross because God was angry, but rather because God is not willing that any—not willing that a single being—should perish (2 Peter 3:9), and through his death on the cross everyone and everything is reconciled to God (Colossians 1:20).

Here is the best news we can ever hear: God is not mad at us; God is madly in love with us! Jesus's love is a revelation that he was willing to do whatever it took to restore us to a right relationship with God, with others, and with ourselves. The depth and extent of God's love revealed to us in Jesus is beyond measure and more than we can imagine.

Prayer: God, I cannot fathom your love, but I can experience it. Amen.

Week Forty-three, Day 1

Read John 13:17

John 13:17 rolled Jesus's actions about love and his teachings on love into one occasion, his evening with the disciples in an upper room in Jerusalem, just before he was betrayed. It is very important to note that he made love the central message to his followers.

He began with an action, washing the disciples' feet, and telling them he had given them an example of love that he wanted them to follow (13:1-20). It was not so much a ceremony to be repeated as it was a spirit of servanthood he wanted them to personify.

He then moved to teach them about love, but not in the abstract. He told his disciples to love "as I have loved you" (13:34). They knew how to love because they knew how he had loved them, and others. We will turn to some of his lessons on love in John 15.

And finally, he prayed for them and for all who would come to believe in him. It was a love prayer (17:24-26). The whole occasion was about love.

Prayer: God, Jesus made it clear—it's all about love. Amen.

Week Forty-three, Day 2

Read 1 Corinthians 13:1-13

Jesus's example of love and his teaching about it shaped his first followers. But it was not always the defining way, nor was it equally applied in the body of Christ. The Corinthian church was such a place. So, in his first letter to the congregation, he included what we call "the love chapter." We will turn our attention to it, exploring Paul's message in detail.

Today we look at the chapter in its larger context, noting that it comes between two chapters dealing with spiritual gifts. The two chapters can almost be read without going through chapter 13 . . . almost. Except for the fact that Paul put the love chapter between them. Why?

A look at the first eleven chapters provides a clue. The Corinthians were genuine Christians, but they were making a lot of mistakes, many of them due to a lack of love. Paul could imagine them messing up spiritual gifts for lack of love. He headed that problem off at the pass.

Prayer: God, so much goes off the rails when love is absent. Keep me on track by keeping me in love with you and with others. Amen.

Week Forty-three, Day 3

Read 1 Corinthians 13:1-3

Spiritual gifts can so easily be contaminated by prideful comparison (e.g., "my gifts are better than yours"), that Paul makes it plain, we can have all the gifts of the Spirit, and a whole lot more—but if we lack love, we have nothing, Nothing, NOTHING.

He makes his point by proposing seven superlative lifestyles (none of which any of us would ever dream to be possible), and says that if we had any of them—or even all of them—without love we would be nothing, Nothing, NOTHING.

Any questions? Even in Corinth where pride so often took over (even in the church), there would be no questions, only silence. And that's where we have to come to if we are to be genuine in our faith and Christian in our conduct. These three verses are Jesus's first beatitude put into different words. "Any questions?" Paul asks. Then and now, we say "n. It is in such silence and absence of hubris that love can germinate, take root, and grow.

Prayer: God, I get it. Now let it get me. Amen.

Week Forty-three, Day 4

Read 1 Corinthians 13:4

Patience is a positive attribute in general. In a world where speed has become an expectation, it is too often in short supply. But the word Paul used in the Greek is more than having patience with airplane schedules and other circumstances. In fact, it is not a word about having patience with things beyond our control.

The patience Paul is describing is being patient with people. It is not being hard-nosed with people when they fail to deliver, fulfill expectations, or meet deadlines. It is being patient when we have every right not to be. It is choosing to be patient rather than angry. It is the kind of patience God has with us (2 Peter 3:9). When God's love is in our hearts, it is the kind of patience we will give to others.

Patience creates space for the whole story to emerge. When it does, we often find people were not deliberately disappointing, but rather were dealing with things that rendered them late or unsatisfactory. Patience is sometimes what another person needs to recover.

Prayer: God, let me be patient with others the way you are with me. Amen.

Week Forty-three, Day 5

Read 1 Corinthians 13:4

Kindness is a virtue in its own right, but it is often the package in which our patience is wrapped. Someone has said, "Be kind to others. You never know what they are going through."

Today, we might refer to this as not being mean-spirited. You would think that Paul would not have to tell Christians to be kind. But in his day, and all the way up to ours, there are Christians who are not kind. They have an edge about them. John Wesley called it "sour godliness," and went on to say it is the devil's religion.

Kindness is another word for compassion, love that is tender—love that lifts people up, encourages them, and renews their strength. We leave the presence of a kind person better than when we came. We say of kind people, "they do me good," and we mean it figuratively and literally. It was the way of Jesus (Acts 10:38). It is the way whenever love prevails.

Prayer: God, soften my spirit so that I do not live with a hard heart. Amen.

Week Forty-four, Day 1

Read 1 Corinthians 13:4

Love is not jealous. After declaring two positive things about love (patient and kind), Paul commences an eightfold description of its negativity, beginning with envy.

Paul does not say why he began there, but I think it is because jealousy is the disease that eats away at us often without anyone else knowing. Of course, there are outward manifestations of jealousy, but by the time others see them, we are goners. Paul says that the worst thing about being unloving is that it destroys our soul before it harms anyone else's. In fact, we can be jealous and look like we are religious. Envy burns from the inside out.

The sadness of jealousy like this is that it is death by comparison. Our lives are not defined by what others have. Envy is the sign that we are "beside ourselves" bearing a grudge rather than "in our right mind" giving a blessing. When another's good fortune makes us angry, we have ceased to love.

Prayer: God, let what others have become a song in my heart, not a stone in my spirit. Amen.

Week Forty-four, Day 2

Read 1 Corinthians 13:4

Love does not brag. Bragging is a sign of jealousy. Because we are envious of another's good fortune, our ego launches a game of "one up." Being king of the hill is what jealousy is all about. Bragging is one way to claim higher ground.

We brag with more than our allegations. We brag with our appearances where "my _____ is better than your _____" is standard fare. It can be anything. But one thing it is not: it is not love.

Why? Because agape rejoices in the other person. Love celebrates the other, not itself. Love enjoys marching in someone else's parade. When we love, we find that some of the happiest moments in our lives are when we share in someone else's joy.

Prayer: God, I want to live so that I enjoy the show, not steal it. Amen.

Week Forty-four, Day 3

Read 1 Corinthians 13:4

Love is not arrogant. It is not filled with itself. Bragging on the outside comes from being puffed up on the inside. The problem with puff is that it's mostly air. That's why we call arrogant people windbags.

Arrogance is "all fluff and no stuff," arising from the simple fact that it uses itself to define itself. In social parlance it means we have "not gotten out enough" to realize we are not the only game in town. Arrogance is ingrownness.

Now is a good time to remind ourselves that Paul chose descriptions of love, and the lack of it, in relation to the Corinthian Christians—that part of the body of Christ that had become arrogant. They had given themselves an Oscar for "Best Christians" forgetting no one else but them voted. In this sense, arrogance is the easiest fault to have because we only have to convince ourselves that we're number one.

Prayer: God, save me from arrogance by filling me with your Spirit, so that I don't fill myself with me. Amen.

Week Forty-four, Day 4

Read 1 Corinthians 13:5

Love isn't rude. It does not accept bluntness and brutality as virtuous. Sadly, there is a version of Christianity that "tells it like it is," with little thought as to how the message comes across or the consequences (e.g., shaming) that goes along with it.

Paul says that this is faux love. Love is not mean-spirited or crude. True love always expresses itself with a graciousness that keeps the fruit of the Spirit in play (Galatians 5:22-23).

There are times when the biblical message comes through in the most ordinary thing. This is one of those times. It is the message of civility and courtesy. This is not diminishing the gospel; it is the reminder that God's will and way is expressed in the our ordinary attitudes and actions. If love does not come through in our routines, there's no basis for believing it will be present in our exceptions. The message is clear: love is shown in our ordinary activities with winsomeness.

Prayer: God, I want my love to be an uplift, not a putdown. Amen.

Week Forty-four, Day 5

Read 1 Corinthians 13:5

Love is not self-seeking. Whenever we begin with a "what's in it for me?" attitude, we know we are not living from love. To start with "my rights" poisons the ego so that we fail to recognize our responsibilities. From a psychological/developmental standpoint, we are spoiled brats masquerading as adults.

Here is where a reminder is in order about the kind of love Paul is commending: agape. The defining quality is that it does not seek its own good, but rather the good of others.

Common good is the only goodness that enriches the whole. Every other kind creates a have/have not world. In agape everyone prospers; every other way advances the few at the expense of the many. This is not God's way. It must not be ours. Where love prevails, everyone thrives.

Prayer: God, if I live in love, I will never be the only one in the picture. Amen.

Week Forty-five, Day 1

Read 1 Corinthians 13:5

Love is not irritable. That is, it is not touchy or "thin skinned." Love does not live on the edge, with a one-strike-and-you're-out mentality. Knee-jerk reactions are the fuel that enflames anger. The older brother in Jesus's parable of the prodigal son is an example of irritability on display, to the extent that he would not welcome his brother home—an irritability that prevented him from attending the party.

Irritability is an indication that perfectionism has infected our soul. People who are easily offended and who are never satisfied cannot love as God intends because they enter into relationships with expectations/demands that no one can fulfill. Bitterness is the outcome of unreality. Judgmentalism is a grudge, not a virtue.

True love is always expressed in reality, and the reality is that life is not fair. Others will disappoint us. Things do not always go our way. True love rolls with the punch and weathers the storm.

"My way or the highway" only comes from those who need to hit the road.

Prayer: God, soften my heart so that I do not place burdens on people that they cannot carry. Amen.

Week Forty-five, Day 2

Read 1 Corinthians 13:5

Love does not keep a record of wrongs. Unloving people have a sick knack for being able to recount all the ways they have been hurt or mistreated by others. Their go-to reaction is to pull up the list, read it, and reelect themselves presidents of the "Poor Me Club."

We must guard against becoming one who cannot let something go. To hold on is to continue plotting how to get even down the road. Love dies in the atmosphere of revenge. And worse, keeping a scorecard of wrongs means that we tend to lash out at those who had nothing to do with the offense in the first place. We can go so far into this that any target will do, and we harm others with our resentments.

Love does not deny being wronged, nor does it subject itself to further abuse. Love has the courage to protect itself, but not with the motive of retaliation defining our actions.

Prayer: God, give me the grace not to have my memories erased, but rather to have them healed. Amen.

Week Forty-five, Day 3

Read 1 Corinthians 13:6

Love is not happy with injustice. This is a stand-alone characteristic to go along with the previous ones. In another sense, it is a summary of them all. *Injustice* is the word used when others do not receive what they should. Injustice is deprivation. All the previous "love is not" descriptions are deprivations of one kind or another.

Before Paul pivots to say what love is, he gathers it all up with an overarching message: love never exists at someone else's expense. When anyone is denied decency in general or something in particular that they should have, love is absent.

That's why nonviolent resistance is ignited and sustained by love. Love is just—that is, it seeks the common good. It refuses to look the other way when it is not provided. Here is the prophetic dimension of love: refusing to be silent and passive when the common good is denied. Love is the force for good that comes from God's heart into ours, moving us to endure in the ministry of overcoming evil with good.

Prayer: God, never let me settle for injustice . . . never. Amen.

Week Forty-five, Day 4

Read 1 Corinthians 13:6

Love rejoices in the truth. Here is the pivot where Paul turns to what love is and what it does. And the first thing he mentions is that love is happy with the truth.

Note that it is a continuation of the previous item, but now in a positive way. By making the connection, Paul makes it clear that the kind of truth he has in mind is not a concept; it's a conduct. If injustice (denial of the common good) is not love, then true love is justice. Truth is the establishment of the common good. Truth is an activation, not an affirmation.

Unfortunately, too much Christianity has deteriorated into concepts (creeds, doctrines) to be believed, when it is meant to be conducts to be behaved. The big phrase for it is sapiential theology: truth that is experienced and expressed, not just affirmed and professed. Love is lived theology. Love is the theology God has in mind and the kind the world is longing for. Truth is love incarnate, love in action.

Prayer: God, give me the hands and feet of love while giving me a heart of love. Give me love for the road. Amen.

Week Forty-five, Day 5

Read 1 Corinthians 13:7

Love puts up with all things. This does not mean that love accepts everything or continues to be victimized by it. The word is *bears* and it is a word of strength, not weakness; a word of action, not passivity. It is a word that describes load-bearing capacity.

We call it tenacity. It is being determined or persuaded. We bear all things through the strength of our convictions. Paul described it as being convinced that nothing can separate us from the love of God in Christ Jesus (Romans 8:38-39). This kind of tenacity generates joy as we "bear up" in order to "carry on." It is the joy Jesus exemplified when he accepted the cross (Hebrews 12:2).

Putting up with all things does not minimize the weight of them. We feel everything as it is. And sometimes, the struggle and pain bring us to the breaking point. And yet, by God's grace, we do not break. We "bear up" and keep going.

Prayer: God, I seek your strength to carry the load, whatever it may be. Amen.

Week Forty-six, Day 1

Read 1 Corinthians 13:7

Love trusts in all things. This does not mean everything is trustworthy. It means that God's will and way is never totally conquered by anything. In relation to God, we live by the conviction that we are never alone. God is with us: Immanuel. In relation to people, we live by the conviction that no one is devoid of goodness. The image of God is in everyone.

Admittedly, both of these things are difficult to see when we are in the midst of challenges and sufferings. In the heat of the moment, God seems to be absent and people appear to be evil. It takes another vision to see things differently. It takes trust.

Love believes the best about God and others, not out of naivete, but on the basis of revelation. God is shown to be with us always (Psalm 23:4; Matthew 28:20), and even the worst people can still change. We love on the basis of our convictions, not our circumstances.

Prayer: God, calibrate my soul by convictions, not my circumstances. Amen.

Week Forty-six, Day 2

Read 1 Corinthians 13:7

Love hopes for all things. Nothing and no one are hopeless. Paul said as much in the last admonition. Here he says it again. Why?

Because we tend to typecast and pigeonhole people. But the truth is, everyone is a work in progress. We claim that to be true for ourselves; we must believe it is true of others as well.

Given the extent to which people can go to be stupid and mean, it is easy to believe they are lost causes. But that is to confuse a photograph with a motion picture. A person may be anything in a given moment (or even for a long time), but it does not mean they will be that way forever. Interestingly, that is why some Christians believe everyone will be saved. They do not believe anyone can resist God's love and grace eternally. And the fact is, a lot of people do have a change of heart before they die (and who knows about afterward?), so we keep on loving hopefully.

Prayer: God, you never give up on anyone. Help me do the same. Amen.

Week Forty-six, Day 3

Read 1 Corinthians 13:7

Love endures all things. In a nutshell it means love wins. Love has the final word, so it does not cave in, evaporate, or run away in the face of evil. Evil is not immortal; love is. Vice is not eternal; virtue is. Original goodness, not original sin, defines the story. And so, we endure. We say with hymn writer Maltbie Babcock, "Though the wrong seems oft so strong, God is the ruler yet."[41] We march with those who sing, "We shall overcome someday."

Endurance is a short-term action based upon a long-term conviction. It is allowing the light of an anticipated victory to illuminate our path of present reality. Endurance is having enough light to take the next step. Endurance does not mean we are always winning; it means we are never quitting. We keep on keeping on.

Prayer: God, give me the will to enact my convictions in the short run because I envision them for the long haul. Amen.

Week Forty-six, Day 4

Read 1 Corinthians 13:8

Love never fails. It does not mean we never fail. We do. But love does not fail. Love is our home. The light is always on, and we can return. That's the story, and Jesus made it plain in the three stories he told in Luke 15.

It is altogether possible that we may have misunderstood hell. We treat it like it is a place of eternal punishment, but it may be a state of eternal correction, the unending process of God's redeeming love. The phrase usually translated "eternal punishment" in Matthew 25:46 can also mean "eternal correction," and Christians across the centuries have understood Jesus's statement that way.

Love never fails means God never turns out the light and locks the door . . . never. God never gives up on us . . . never. Love continues to search until every sheep and coin is found, until every person is home. Luke described this kind of love in Acts 3:21. Paul wrote about it in Ephesians 1:9-10. God's love never fails, never ceases. And when God's love is in our hearts, we never give up either.

Prayer: God, you always keep the light in your home on for people. Give me grace to keep it on in my heart for others too. Amen.

Week Forty-six, Day 5

Read 1 Corinthians 13:8-12

In these verses Paul is setting the stage for his big finish with respect to love. He highlights certain things that we often substitute for love, saying that we must not rely on any of them because they will not last.

Paul says we must not allow religion or self-sufficiency to supersede love. Prophecies, tongues, and knowledge are always partial. They are also transient. In and of themselves they are incomplete and insufficient. Why? Because they are essentially nonrelational. We can be either religious or smart, or both, and still be unloving. Paul is reminding us of what he said in verses 1-3.

These verses may seem far removed from our time, but they speak powerfully to us. We are always tempted to substitute things for love. But whatever we put in the place of love is a paltry substitute. Paul makes it clear that when "the perfect comes"—that is, when the final story is written, it will be the story of love. We will not be judged by how spiritual or intelligent we were, but whether or not we were loving.

Prayer: God, instill in me the one thing that lasts forever: love. Amen.

⚊⚌

Week Forty-seven, Day 1

Read 1 Corinthians 13:13—14:1

Faith, hope, and love remain. They do not pass away. We will forever exhibit trust, confidence, and affection. But of these three, the greatest is love.

Why? Because love is the basis for our faith and our hope. Love defines the essence of faith and hope. With respect to faith, love sums up the two Great Commandments. With respect to hope, love prevails.

We cannot know what existence fully defined by love will be, but through Paul's words we are assured that such a world will be. Eternity is summed up in one word: *love*.

So, dipping into the next chapter, Paul says, "Pursue love." We are to make love our aim each day that we live. We exist to love God and others. That's it. Doing this sets the trajectory for how we will live forever. Love is the essence of the mystery we call heaven.

Prayer: God, may your singular will be my ultimate goal. Amen.

Week Forty-seven, Day 2

Read 1 John 3:11

About forty years after Paul wrote his love chapter, John wrote two of his own. Paul commended the excellency of love; John described the expression of it. We turn to what John adds to the picture in this next round of meditations.

As we move from 1 Corinthians into 1 John, it is important to note that both are written to Christian communities, which is to remind ourselves that love is concrete, not abstract. Love is expressed, not just professed; behaved, not just believed. The excellency of love is confirmed by experience.

It is also worth seeing that love is not automatic; it is a choice. It was lacking in both Corinth and Ephesus. And more, it was lacking among the very people you'd expect it to be present: Christians.

Things have not changed. That's why these weeks of meditations are so important.

Prayer: God, let me never forget that the life of love is not only your offer, it is my choice. Amen.

Week Forty-seven, Day 3

Read 1 John 2:5

John focuses on love in chapters 3, 4, and 5 of his letter. But the first mention of it is here. To understand the specifics that John presents, we must see them in the context John offers in this verse. The context is obedience.

Love is an act, not just an attitude. The details John goes into a bit later are expressions of this basic truth. We cannot say we are loving people if we do not love people. Others are our brothers and sisters (2:9-11; 3:14-18), and John is not limiting this sense of family to Christians loving other Christians, but rather calling us to love everyone as siblings in one human family.

Unless we see this, we will find slippery ways to avoid the details about love that John provides in his letter. We are to act lovingly toward everyone. John is only passing on what Jesus and Paul previously said. It is now our turn to pass the same message on in our day.

Prayer: God, I will pass on the message I have received—that I am to love everyone, for every person is my sibling in the human family. Amen.

Week Forty-seven, Day 4

Read 1 John 2:15

John offers another big-picture look at love before diving into the details: love is counterintuitive and countercultural. It is the opposite of craving.

Our Buddhist friends have studied "wrong desire" more deeply than many Christians. They conclude it is the root from which the rest of evil comes. We believe the same thing, calling it original sin. We crave to be our own gods and to gratify our desires at the expense of our siblings in the human family.

Craving is the antithesis of love. As Paul wrote, love does not insist on its own way (1 Corinthians 13:5). Rather, love is generous, serving, and compassionate. Love is other-oriented. Before John goes into detail about love, he establishes its disposition—to seek and work for the common good. By doing this, John linked love to the justice message running through the Bible. Love is how we act in order to restore life as God intends for it to be.

Prayer: God, I set my navigation system by love, so that I may go in the direction you would have me go. Amen.

Week Forty-seven, Day 5

Read 1 John 3:1

We love as we do for one simple reason: we are God's children, not just in name but in nature. God is love (4:8, 16). Made by God, we will be lovers too.

Love springs from more than our will, or even our inclination. It springs from our creation in the image of God. We are like God in many ways. The chief way is that we are made to love. Like Creator, like children.

Failure to love is not only an unfortunate omission, it is a fundamental violation. It is not merely a failure to act, it is a failure to be. We are God's children.

But there is more. Using the word *children*, John is saying we can grow in love. With that idea in place, he is ready to dive into the details of what that looks like in everyday living. The rest of our meditations on John's letter focus on our maturation love.

Prayer: God, I am your beloved child. I am not only like you, I can become more and more like you. That's what I want to be. Amen.

❦

Week Forty-eight, Day 1

Read 1 John 3:13-19

After referring to love among other things in the first two chapters of his letter, John makes love his singular focus for most of the remainder of it. He does not specifically state why he concentrates on love, but we can assume it is a combination of John's conviction that love is the essence and apex of faith, and his observation that the Christian community needed to grow in love.

For John, we learn what love is not by beginning with the metaphysics of it (that is, the philosophical aspects of it), but rather with the materiality of it (that is, physical aspects of it). We learn what love is by loving one another (v. 14). So, we must not love "words or speech but with actions and truth" (v. 18). Love is a verb; it's what we do.

This love, John wrote, is illustrated in Jesus as he laid down his life for people, and his love-in-action life must be the way we live as well. In practical terms this means the validity of our love is not that we claim to be loving, but that others feel loved by us. Love is confirmed by conduct, not creed; by behavior, not belief.

Prayer: God, I wish never to say I love others without them feeling loved by me. Amen.

Week Forty-eight, Day 2

Read 1 John 3:20-24

Much of our faith is paradox—that is, we receive something that's the opposite of what we are saying or doing. And so it is with love. When we express our love to others, we experience God's love in ourselves.

True love is always paradoxical. We increase it by giving it away. We thrive inwardly when we help others to live well. This is not so when we start with self-love because the ego is never satisfied. It always wants more, and we end up claiming to be loving without actually being so. Love that begins with us does not reach others because we consume it on ourselves. Paradoxically, we experience love as we express it.

The principle is this: "give, and it will be given to you" (Luke 6:38). Loving evokes our sense of being loved. We hand out love, not merely hang out with it. We give it away, and we gain more than if we had kept it to ourselves.

Prayer: God, I want to experience your love. Help me do it your way, by expressing it to others. Amen.

Week Forty-eight, Day 3

Read 1 John 4:1-6

The word *love* does not appear in these verses, but John has not changed the subject. He is looking at love from a different angle. We "test the spirits" by whether or not we "confess Christ" (v. 2).

But what Christ are we confessing? John has made this clear. We confess the Christ of love (3:16). Or as the hymn puts it, "they will know we are Christian by our love." Love is the way we tell whether or not we are Christians, and the way we tell if others are. This is not being judgmental (because we apply the same criterion to ourselves); it is "fruit inspection." That is, if we claim to bear the fruit of love, it should be visible on the branches of our lives. If others claim to be Christian, the fruit of love should be observable in their lives as well.

John Wesley said the same thing, "Sour godliness is the devil's religion." So, John said: test the spirit. If love is there, Christianity is too. If love is absent, so is Christianity.

Prayer: God, I will use one basis for seeing whether Christianity is present or absent in me or in others: love. Amen.

Week Forty-eight, Day 4

Read 1 John 4:7-11

In these verses, John expands his exhortation that we are to "confess Christ" by our love by saying we are to love sacrificially. The life of love is not minimalism, it is investing in the promotion of the well-being of others. Love does not ask, "What's the least I can do?" but rather "What is called for?"

Paul helps us here. He said we are "a living sacrifice" (Romans 12:1). Living sacrifices keep on giving. Sacrificial love is love for the long haul. Jesus illustrated such love in the parable of the good Samaritan (Luke 10:30-37), which was a story meant to teach what the second Great Commandment (loving our neighbor as ourselves) is all about. But he did more; he incarnated such love by giving his life for us.

In today's passage John has expanded the depth and breadth of love—God's love for us, and our love for others. It is summed up in one word: *sacrificial*. "If God loved us this way, we also ought to love one another."

Prayer: God, I will not define love by minimums or moments, but by investments and journeys. Amen.

Week Forty-eight, Day 5

Read 1 John 4:12-16

The kind of love John is describing is from God through the Spirit (v. 13). Love is the fruit of the Spirit (Galatians 5:22-23). Fruit exists to be eaten. Love exists to be shared.

The sharing of love is the way the world is saved, in time and for eternity. In time, love produces the redemption and lift of society. Where love prevails, everyone and everything thrives. The new creation is the restoration of love.

Love is described in terms of fullness. It is to be filled with the fullness of God, who is love (Ephesians 3:19-21). Jesus said he came to fulfill the law (Matthew 5:17)—that is, to "fill it full" with what is always lacking in legalism: love. The Great Commission is not summed up in the word *evangelism*, but rather in the word *love*. To make disciples is to make lovers—lovers of God and lovers of others. That's why Tertullian sought to prove the validity of Christianity by saying, "See how they love each other."

Prayer: God, I will prove love is real by sharing it. Amen.

❧

Week Forty-nine, Day 1

Read 1 John 4:16-18

One of the most remarkable passages in the Bible is found in today's reading, "we are exactly the same as God is in this world."

That's the kind of statement that can do us good or do us in. We must understand it.

Clearly we are not like God in every respect, but we are like God in one respect: in love. When we live, we are doing in the world exactly what God is doing.

John says that loving is the way we know we are on the right track—the way we have confidence. Whatever final judgment there is, it is not one we fear. There is no fear when we are weighed on the scale of love. Love casts out fear. We live with confidence with respect to time and eternity when we live lives of love.

Prayer: God, I have no fear because I have love. Amen.

Week Forty-nine, Day 2

Read 1 John 4:19

This verse puts everything John is saying into perspective. Any claims we make to be loving people stand upon a prior revelation: we love because God first loved. God's love has been poured into our heart. Our love is the overflow of that love. We are not creators of love; we are conduits of love—God's love.

Saint Francis used the word *instrument* to describe it. Bernard of Clairvaux used the word *reservoir*. Both metaphors convey the same message—the water does not originate with us, and it is not meant to remain in us. That is exactly what John is saying.

If you go to the Holy Land, you will visit the Dead Sea. It is a geological illustration of the biblical truth that the spiritual life must have both inflow and outflow. The sea does not make the water, and it is not meant to hold on to it. The same is true of us. We love because God first loved us.

Prayer: God, I ask for your love, not only that I might receive it but also that I might pass it on. Amen.

Week Forty-nine, Day 3

Read 1 John 4:20-21

The spiritual life is one of congruence. Our words and deeds must match. When they do not, our deeds (not our words) tell the true story of who we are.

There is not a Christian in the world who claims to be unloving. We all say that we love God and others. But the actions of some Christians show that their claim is bogus.

As John drew near to the end of his letter, he returned to the love of "brothers and sisters" (fellow human beings) as the litmus test of our faith. He lays the profession of faith lying in the dust when it is not confirmed by action. Genuine Christianity exists when our attitudes and actions are in sync. Until they are, John says we are blowing smoke.

Prayer: God, I seek to be love, not just talk about love. Amen.

Week Forty-nine Day 4

Read 1 John 5:1-3a

Our testimony to love must be proven by our enacting of it. That is, we keep God's commandments, gathered together into two: loving God and loving others. We cannot claim to be lovers of God if we are not lovers of others (4:20).

John used the analogy of parenthood to make the point. If we love the parent, we love the child of the parent. In fact, our love of the parent is confirmed by our love of the child.

The gospel is clear: God has made all people. We are meant to love all people. Full stop. Some Christians are denying this. The failure to love everyone produced faux faith. Full stop.

This assessment is not judgmental, it is biblical. It is taking John's message and applying it in the present.

Prayer: God, let me never default on the one simple fact that the love of all is the only kind of genuine love there is. Amen.

Week Forty-nine, Day 5

Read 1 John 5:3b

John's final word about love is one we must not miss: living the life of love (i.e., keeping God's commandments) is not difficult.

The fact is, it takes more time to devise evil than it does to do justice. It takes more effort to do harm than to do good. It takes more energy to hate than it does to love. That's why those who do not love end up being critical, bitter, narcissistic, angry, fearful, and self-righteous. The lack of love has drained them of life. It shows.

But so too does showing love. It shows in the manifestation of the fruit of the Spirit. It shows in the lightness of being. It shows in the sense that life is wonderful. It shows in the way it attracts others and includes them in the dance.

John's final message is that the Christian life is not a burden, it's a blessing. It is not an obligation, it is an opportunity. It is not a duty, it is a delight. It shows.

Prayer: God, not loving and loving both show. I choose to show love. Amen.

❧❧

Week Fifty, Day 1

Read Deuteronomy 6:4

We are living in a time of Awakening. The final round of meditations will focus on this, but in a real sense, every meditation in this book is in this context and written to help us be people who advance the Awakening where we are and as we are.

Awakenings are times of gathering. They are times of coming back together around the eternal Grand Story. They are times when the Big Picture is seen. In religion this is referred to as the Perennial Tradition. It is what we might call "religion before there were religions." We will look at key aspects of it this week.[42]

We begin with singularity of God. God is one, as today's reading reminds us. There is not a Jewish God and a Hindu God, a Methodist God and a Baptist God. There is one God who has made all that exists and within whom all things exist (Acts 17:28). We are called to announce the Oneness of God, for it in this Oneness that we remember our oneness with everyone and everything.

Prayer: God, in your Singularity I find my life. Amen.

Week Fifty, Day 2

Read Romans 11:33

In the Grand Story we discover that the one God is Mystery. Who God is and what God does is beyond our complete knowing. This does not mean we know nothing about God, it means that what we know comes from God to us. We call it revelation.

Far from being a disappointment, Paul says it is a deep and rich revelation. We know this is true as we discover more about God's person and presence in all things, from the smallest particle to the farthest star. But even with all we know, the final word is *Mystery.*

This is essential, not only because of God's eternality, but also because of our ego. The spiritual life must be humble. Otherwise, it gets hijacked by egotism. Mystery is the means for keeping the

God/human difference intact. Mystery delivers the saving message to us, "I am God, and you are not."

Prayer: God, expand my sense of Mystery. It is where I find you, find myself, find life. Amen.

Week Fifty, Day 3

Read Psalm 42:1

The Grand Story moves on to say that we hunger to be in relationship with God. Communion is the result of creation. The God who is understood to be relational (i.e., Trinity) desires to be in relationship with us. Our hunger for God is the magnet that draws our "iron-filing" soul into the relationship.

That's why Mystery is so important. Without it, the ego attempts to convince us that the hunger we feel is for materialism, hedonism, and power. The ego tempts us to settle for too little, to seek life in things that pass away.

The hunger we feel at the deepest level is the hunger for God. It is a hunger as intense and incessant as a deer's thirst for water. And as the deer, our hunger for God is natural, built into us in our very nature. The hunger to know and to be known by God is the heart of the spiritual life.

Prayer: God, I see that the hunger for life that I feel is my hunger for you. I will satisfy my hunger in you, not in lesser things. Amen.

Week Fifty, Day 4

Read Psalm 139:14

The Grand Story culminates in the truth that we are made for this reality. We are made for God (e.g., Genesis 1:26-27). This is not a repetition of emerging truth; it is the basis for it.

The spiritual life is natural. It is intrinsic to our nature. It is not an addition to our lives, it is the essence of them. It is the life God intends for us all, making all of us in the image of God.

That's why Jesus said the kingdom of God is within us (Luke 17:21). His metaphors were ones of nearness, not distance. His message was that we live here-and-now, not there-and-later. Jesus's invitation is to dive in, not defer, summed up in two words "Follow me" (Mark 1:17).

We are made for this. As the psalmist puts it, we are reverently and marvelously made for this. We are never more at home than when we are in God's house. That house is one we live right now. "Now is the day of salvation" (2 Corinthians 6:2).

Prayer: God, like the lungs are made for air, I am made for you. Your Spirit is my oxygen. I breathe! Amen.

Week Fifty, Day 5

Read Mark 2:22

About every five hundred years, we go through a new Awakening.[43] We are in one today. The wine of God is being poured into new wineskins.

This book emerges from the conviction that we are living in a time when God is doing a new thing. Our call is to recognize it, respond to it, and become those who are instruments of God for advancing it (Isaiah 43:19). The meditations are intentionally aimed to subvert a "business as usual" mindset. They are meant to eliminate sacred cows and the fallen-world imperialism they produce.

This was the mission of Jesus. If we say we follow him, it must be our mission too.

Prayer: God, I get it. I'm in! Amen.

Week Fifty-one, Day 1

Read 2 Corinthians 5:17-18

As we head into the homestretch of these meditations, I want to use this week's meditations to focus on some of the "life" passages that mean the most to me—the ones that have been key in my spiritual formation. There are more than five, but five this week will have to suffice.

I return to the passage that has been with me since I professed my faith in Christ in 1963. Paul's words gave me the vision for the life I had committed myself to live: the new creation. E. Stanley Jones expanded that vision to mean life "in Christ," and more recently Matthew Fox and Richard Rohr have helped me see the significance of the cosmic/universal Christ that Jones helped me see in his description of the excarnate/incarnate Christ.

Additionally, Paul's words helped me see that life in Christ is a journey—one that includes struggle (the old having to pass away in order for the new to come), and one that gives us the grace to engage in the ministry of reconciliation. It has taken decades for this to unfold in my life, and I am still only a Christian in the making.

Prayer: God, thank you for using Paul to get me going. Amen.

Week Fifty-one, Day 2

Read John 15

There are passages of Scripture that, if we only had them, would largely describe the spiritual life. This chapter is one of them. Add the rest of John's Gospel and his three letters, and we have the makings of a feast that will nourish us all our days.

Like Paul, John says everything is found in Christ, who is full of grace and truth (John 1:14). Because that is so, we have one task: to abide in Christ as a branch abides in a vine. Out of this abiding, we bear fruit—fruit in abundance, fruit that remains.

The fruit we bear is love, as Jesus makes clear in today's reading. Love is the fruit of the Spirit, manifesting itself in the eight additional words in Galatians 5:22-23. We live in Christ to the extent we live in love. Amazingly, living the life of love, we will incur opposition from "the world"—from the individual and collective false self that prefers darkness to light (John 3:19). But we press on.

Prayer: God, I will live the life of love when it is easy or difficult—whether others like it or not. Amen.

Week Fifty-one, Day 3

Read Psalm 23

The older I get, the more meaningful this psalm becomes. When I recited it as a child in church and later as a new follower of Christ, I had not had to walk through the valley of the shadow of death or feast at God's table of plenty in the presence of enemies. I have now.

And doing so, I understand how goodness and mercy follow us all the days of our lives. We are never alone, never left to face our perils by ourselves. God is with us. Emmanuel. The Good Shepherd, whose goodness and mercy have followed me all the days of my life.

And more, as an older adult with less of a path ahead of me than behind me, I claim the hope given to me in this psalm, "and I will dwell in the house of the Lord for ever" (KJV). I live in this psalm without fear. In God there are no "disposable" people or things. I am heading for a life where every knee bows and everyone is made alive in Christ (1 Corinthians 15:22) and every tongue confesses that Jesus Christ is Lord (Philippians 2:11). Life is wonderful in time and for eternity.

Prayer: God, you are my Shepherd. I am your sheep. How cool! Amen.

Week Fifty-one, Day 4

Read Matthew 5–7

It's impossible to leave the Sermon on the Mount off any list of key formative passages. Countless Christians, non-Christians, and even people with no religious affiliation say, "My religion is the Sermon on the Mount."

Why? There's more than one reason, I am sure. Today I point to John Wesley's comment that the Sermon on the Mount is a holiness primer. The life God intends for us is encapsulated in Jesus's message. That's true with respect to inward and outward holiness, personal and social holiness. The Sermon on the Mount describes the essence of the spiritual life.

E. Stanley Jones rightly notes (as did Wesley) that Matthew 5:48 is the mountain peak verse, where Jesus taught that our love is to be complete (that is, for everyone and everything) just as God's love is. In short, we turn to the Sermon on the Mount to know what the spiritual life is, how to live it, and to do so with the assurance that we will be given the grace to do so.

Prayer: God, the Sermon on the Mount is your laser beam for living as you intend. I see the light. I feel the power. I accept the invitation. Amen.

Week Fifty-one, Day 5

Read Genesis 1–2

I end this summary week at the largest place, at the panoramic vantage point: the creation. In the two metaphorical stories about it, we see how God made life to be, and what the restoration of it will look like.

Through a series of visuals and analogies we discover that all of life (heaven and earth) is sacred (God made), and in that sacredness we are one with everyone and everything. In this oneness life exists on a spectrum that has incalculable diversity (kinds) comprising it in a pervasive network of interbeing. The entire reality is one where God is present in and with all that is. And from the creation story we also learn that there is a pattern and a pace: working and resting.

Later in scripture the creation story is summed up in the word *shalom*—the comprehensive wellness of the cosmos that when integrating and interacting as God intends produces a peace beyond our understanding. In this grandeur, we are God's beloved, made just a little lower than the angels, crowned with glory and honor.

Prayer: God, what a wonderful world you have made. Thank you. Amen.

Week Fifty-two, Day 1

Read Philippians 1:21

In our final week together, I want to thank you for making this yearlong journey. I am aware of your investment merely by knowing you are reading these words, and I am grateful.

But the journey does not end this week. It goes on forever. My responsibility now is to release you from the context of my ideas into those of others. I have decided to place you in the hands of another good guide, Brian McLaren, through his journey book *We Make the Road by Walking*.

I have made this choice (from among other viable candidates) because he uses the metaphor of life to develop his ideas, just as I have used it to communicate mine. *Aliveness* is his word for it. It's a good word. It is what Paul meant in today's reading—what Jesus meant when he said he came to give us abundant life.

Prayer: God, I am alive in you. Amen.

Week Fifty-two, Day 2

Read Psalm 19:1

Last week ended in the creation stories. This is where Brian McLaren begins his book. Creation is both the starting point for life, and it is the reference point for seeing how to recover it. In the deepest and widest sense, the spiritual life is creation spirituality. Today's reading from the Psalms sums it up.

We are alive in the story of creation. That is, we live, move, and have our being in God, who has been creating for 13.8 billion years and is continuing to create. That means we are alive in the story that was (is) alive before we began to live.

Creation ignites awe and wonder in us, along with the necessary humility to corral egotism. Creation illustrates the movement of life, both in its evolution and historicity.

Creation contains the mixture of good and evil, reminding us that abundant living is not automatic or a foregone conclusion. We must choose to live. When we do, we get in sync with the momentum and trajectory of creation, which is light, life, and love.

Prayer: God, I choose life, and in that choice I will move in sync with your creation. Amen.

Week Fifty-two, Day 3

Read Colossians 3:1-3

We are alive in the plentitude of God that we Christians call the Trinity. From God as creator, we move on to speak of life in relation to Christ (excarnate and incarnate) and the Holy Spirit. In God's life we seek a higher way.

The excarnate Christ raises our sights by giving us the confidence that the life of God in the human soul is eternal reality. The incarnate Christ shows us what this life looks like when humans live it. As the Eternal One and the Human One, Christ gives us perspective.

The Holy Spirit elevates our vision as the ever-present means for living the abundant life we have been exploring this past year. The wind of the Spirit fills our sails, empowering, encouraging, and guiding us.

As disciples, we are followers and learners. Discipleship is exploring the heights of revelation God gives us about life and how to live it. Light, life, and love have come to us, inviting us to seek the things that are above.

Prayer: God, you have shown us what life is and how to live it. I accept your invitation to do so. Amen.

Week Fifty-two, Day 4

Read Ephesians 5:18-20

We are pentecostal people, those who are filled with the Spirit. In that fullness we manifest the Spirit's fruit in our character and conduct.

We are living in a time of new Awakening, in a time when the life of God in the human soul is being revived and offered through all who recognize what God is doing and offer themselves as living sacrifices to be instruments through whom God can work to advance abundant life.

It is a global Awakening bringing together people from every place and every religion. It is another uprising by which the old passes away so the new can come. It is a fresh uprising of love, manifesting itself in fresh expressions of faith, community, worship, stewardship, and service. It is an uprising of life (*zoé*) that gives us hope and sets us on the trajectory that will culminate in the restoration of all things in a new heaven and a new earth.

The new Awakening is an advance of the new creation. We can live "in Christ" and offer him to others.

Prayer: God, I will not miss what you are doing on the earth today. Amen.

Week Fifty-two, Day 5

Read Revelation 22:20

These closing words of the cosmic Christ cannot be put on a calendar, but they must be put in our hearts. We end this book of meditations where the Bible ends, with the absolute conviction that God will have the last word. The kingdoms of this world will become the kingdom of God and Christ (Revelation 11:15).

This is our conviction. We live with this hope.

To life!

Prayer: God, I believe this with all my heart. Give me grace to live this with all my heart. Amen.

Meditations in Biblical Order

The meditations in this book are not in biblical order, but the following list arranges them that way. After the book reference (chapter and verse), you will see a week number followed by the day's number. These designations will help you find and reference specific meditations.

Genesis

1–2	51, 5
1:1	41, 1
1:2	34, 2
1:5	18, 2
1:27-28	5, 2
9:1-17	41, 2

Exodus

20:1-17	37, 1
23:9	35,1

Leviticus

19:11	15, 2
19:18	41, 3

Deuteronomy

6:4	41, 3; 50, 1
30:19	35, 3

Joshua

1:3	4, 3
1:5-6	15, 5

Psalms

8:1	4, 5
8:4-5	22, 1
14:2-3	27, 2
19:1	52, 2
23	17, 1-5; 51, 3
27:10	16, 5
31:7	40, 3
34:19	6, 4
37:7-8	5, 4
37:25	1, 2
42:1	50, 3
46:1-3	27, 4
62:5-6	35, 4
100	9, 2
119:105	9, 5
121	41, 4
126:6	4, 2
130	15, 1
139:14	16, 4; 50, 4
142:5	36, 2
146:5-10	2, 2

Proverbs

18:13	3, 2

Ecclesiastes

3:1-8	23, 3

Isaiah

29:13	24, 5
40:1-5	41, 5
41:10-14	27, 5
43:19	36, 4

Jeremiah

6:13-16	16, 1

Lamentations

3:22-23	14, 1

Sirach

1:26	39, 3

Matthew

3:1-2	2, 3
4:12–5:13	25, 1–27, 1
5–7	1, 4
5:17	18, 5
5:21-48	39, 4
6:5-13	31, 1–33, 4
7:7	14, 4

Extended Series

Scattered through this book are some series of meditations that explore a topic for more than one day. You can locate them using the following list:

Exodus 20:1-17, "The Ten Commandments," 37, 1–38, 5

Psalm 8:4; 1 Thessalonians 5:23, "Humanity," 22, 1-5

Psalm 23, "A Portrait of God," 17, 1-5

Matthew 4:17–5:12, "The Blessed Life," 25, 1–26, 5

Matthew 6:5-13; Luke 11:1-4, "True Prayer," 31, 1–33, 5

John 14:6, "Jesus, the Way," 19, 1–21, 5

Acts 2:17-20, "Pentecost," 12, 1–13, 2

1 Corinthians 13, "The Excellency of Love," 43, 2–47, 1

2 Corinthians 5:17-19, "New Creation," 7, 2–8, 5

Galatians 5:22-23, "Fruit of the Spirit," 10, 2–11, 5

1 John 3:11–5:5, "The Life of Love," 47, 2–49, 5

Notes

Foreword

1. Brian D. McLaren, *We Make the Road by Walking* (Nashville: Jericho Books, 2014), xv.

Preface

1. Steve Harper, *Life in Christ: The Core of Intentional Spirituality* (Nashville: Abingdon, 2020).

Introduction

1. Thomas Merton, *New Seeds of Contemplation* (New York: New Directions, 1961), 215.

Daily Meditations

1. Parker Palmer writes about the seasons of our lives in his book *Let Your Life Speak* (San Francisco: Jossey-Bass, 1999), 95–109.

2. Henri Nouwen, *Here and Now: Living in the Spirit* (Pearl River, NY: Crossroad, 1994), 17–18.

3. Thomas Merton, *Conjectures of a Guilty Bystander* (Garden City, NY: Image Books, 1968), 86.

4. John 4:34; 5:19, 30, 36; 8:26, 28-29, 38; 12:49-50; and 14:24.

5. This first name is repeated through the book of Acts 9:2; 18:26; 19:9, 23; 22:4; and 24:14.

6. Thomas Merton, *New Seeds of Contemplation* (New York: New Directions, 1961), 64–69, provides a good overview of his thoughts concerning the self.

7. The phrase is from my wife, Jeannie. It keeps reality and wonder together.

8. I have written more about this in my book *Life in Christ: The Core of Intentional Spirituality* (Nashville: Abingdon, 2020).

9. This is the meaning John Wesley gave to the verse in his *Explanatory Notes upon the New Testament*.

10. Richard Rohr, *Falling Upward* (New York: Jossey-Bass, 2011).

11. Dennis Kinlaw, *We Live as Christ* (Wilmore, KY: Francis Asbury Press, 2001).

12. E. Stanley Jones, *In Christ* (Nashville: Abingdon), 296.

13. Richard Foster explores all six in his book *Streams of Living Water*, rev. ed. (San Francisco: HarperOne, 2001).

14. Amy Carmichael, *Candles in the Dark* (Fort Washington, PA: CLC Publications, 2012), 56.

15. Wesley, *Explanatory Notes upon the New Testament*, comment on Galatians 5:22.

16. This is Lisa Schmidt's guiding word in her Sober Hipster ministry.

17. See the meditation for week 13, day 2.

18. Meditations on the fruit of the Spirit run from week 10, day 2 through week 11, day 5.

19. In addition to this verse, Jesus's disciples are called followers of the Way five more times in Acts: 18:26; 19:9, 23; 22:4; and 24:14. This so important that an extended series on the Way begins next week.

20. In an upcoming reading we will return to the idea of Jesus as the "only" Way.

21. Martin Aronson (*Jesus and Lao-Tzu: The Parallel Sayings* [New York: Seastone, 2003]) provides useful categories for seeing how Jesus and the Tao are related.

22. Richard Hooper, *Jesus, Buddha, Krishna, Lao Tzu: The Parallel Sayings*, 2nd ed. (Sedona, AZ: Thunder Mountain Design and Communications, 2008), 30–43. Here is another good book for seeing the universality of Christ.

23. Cynthia Bourgeault, *The Wisdom Jesus* (Boulder, CO: Shambhala, 2008).

24. Richard Rohr, *Things Hidden: Scripture as Spirituality* (London: SPCK, 2016), 74.

25. John Dear, *The Nonviolent Life* (Corvallis, OR: Pace e Bene Press, 2013).

26. Chapter 4, *Tao Te Ching*, translated by John C. H. Wu, Shambala, 1961.

27. E. Stanley Jones, *The Way* (Nashville: Abingdon, 1946), Sunday, Week 50.

28. E. Stanley Jones, *The Word Became Flesh* (Nashville: Abingdon, 1963), Week 2, Saturday.

29. You can find the complete Covenant Service online by searching "Covenant Renewal Service."

30. Thomas Merton, *Life and Holiness* (Garden City, NY: Image Books, 1963), 22–26.

31. Other pertinent passages include John 12:32; Acts 3:21; Ephesians 1:10; Colossians 1:20.

32. Lewis B. Smedes, *A Pretty Good Person* (New York: HarperCollins, 1991).

33. Robert Fulghum, *Everything I Need to Know I Learned in Kindergarten* (New York: Ivy Books, 1986), 5.

34. This is a prayer phrase that Frank Laubach used in his morning prayers.

35. See the related meditation for Week Thirty, Day 1.

36. Both of the words *monk* and *nun* carry the idea of singular devotion to God.

37. See also Acts 3:21; Colossians 1:18-20, and the verses cited in this meditation.

38. Walter Brueggemann writes about "neighborliness" in many of his books.

39. The sixth "you have heard" (5:43) is not in the Bible. It appears to be something people in the Qumran community were saying. In this way, Jesus showed how commands in scripture or society must be interpreted, not just accepted ipso facto.

40. Rob Bell, *Love Wins* (San Francisco: HarperOne, 2012).

41. Babcock's hymn is "This Is My Father's World."

42. For more, read Bede Griffiths, *Universal Wisdom: A Journey Through the Sacred Wisdom of the World* (New York: Harper-Collins, 1994).

43. Phyllis Tickle, *The Great Emergence: How Christianity Is Changing and Why* (Grand Rapids: Baker, 2012). In a more eclectic way, Andrew Harvey is writing about this in his book *The Direct Path: Personal Journey to the Divine Using the World's Spiritual Traditions* (Easton, PA: Harmony, 2001), and his book with Carolyn Baker, *Radical Regeneration* (Rochester, VT: Inner Traditions, 2022).

Group Meeting Guide

It might seem that a book of meditations has its greatest value in an individual's use of it. And while I do not disagree with that, I also believe that any benefit we receive can be used for the good of others. This book can be used in a group setting as you share the blessings you have received. This guide offers suggestions for doing this in large (class) or small groups.

Large Group Option One: Have the group vote for the meditation that meant the most to them. Then spend the rest of the time in plenary using the pattern below to explore it.

Large Group Option Two: Have the group vote for their favorite meditation, and then divide them into small groups that correspond to their vote (e.g., all the "Wednesday" voters) to explore their choice.

Small Group Option One: Use the Large Group Option One and collectively focus on the chosen passage.

Small Group Option Two: Have each person share their favorite meditation.

Regardless of your group's size, you can follow a general pattern during your time together.

1. Silent centering to prepare, cultivate receptivity, and so forth.

2. Begin with a brief prayer led by an individual or prayed together: "God, be in our midst through our conversation to guide us into ways to embrace and enact the message of our meditations."

3. Ask people to share why they chose the particular meditation. Why was it important to get that message now?

4. Consider specific ways to share the message of the meditation with others in both words and deeds. Let the word become flesh.

5. Encourage silence to allow each person to accept the message and commit to sharing it.

6. Pray the Lord's Prayer together.

For Further Reading

In addition to Brian McLaren's book, *We Make the Road by Walking*, which I commend in Week Fifty-two, I want to recommend some additional resources that cultivate the theme of life. They are all yearlong journeys. I believe we grow best with a long-haul mentality. The resources provide you with that.

Jeff Blake, *A Year on Grace Street*
Walter Brueggemann, *Gift and Task*
Frederick Buechner, *Listening to Your Life*
Oswald Chambers, *My Utmost for His Highest*
Lettie Cowman, *Streams in the Desert*
Richard Foster, *A Year with God*
Matthew Fox, *Christian Mystics: 365 Readings and Meditations*
Irene Hodgson, *Through the Year with Oscar Romero*
E. Stanley Jones, *Abundant Living*
Dennis Kinlaw, *This Day with the Master*
Madeleine L'Engle, *Glimpses of Grace*
C. S. Lewis, *A Year with C. S. Lewis*
Jonathan Montaldo, *A Year with Thomas Merton*
Henri Nouwen, *You Are the Beloved*
Thich Nhat Hanh, *Your True Home*
Eugene Peterson, *Living the Message*

Jan Richardson, *Sacred Journeys*
Alice Russie, *Renew My Heart: Daily Devotional Insights from John Wesley*
William Still, *Through the Year with William Barclay*
Kerry Walters and Robin Jarrell, *Blessed Peacemakers*
Macrina Wiederkehr, *The Flowing Grace of Now*

Other Abingdon Press Books
by Steve Harper

Life in Christ: The Core of Intentional Spirituality
Holy Love: A Biblical Theology for Human Sexuality
Five Marks of a Methodist: The Fruit of a Living Faith
Stepping Aside, Moving Ahead
For the Sake of the Bride

CPSIA information can be obtained
at www.ICGtesting.com
Printed in the USA
LVHW010322200922
728778LV00003B/3